The Tuttle Way

*Applied Methodologies On "How To"
Interpret The Racing Form From A
Winning Horseplayer*

By
Joseph J. Tuttle

Table of Contents

ABOUT THE AUTHOR

Hello, my name is Joseph J Tuttle, and I'm 38 years old. At the ripe old age of ten, the Sun-Sentinel (a Florida based newspaper) did a story about me called..."Does Joey know the score.... Do ya wanna to bet?" I've been a horseplayer ever since I was about 12 years old, so that gives me over a quarter of a century's worth of experience. My Father (Seymour Tuttle) was an owner, trainer, and driver of harness horses. He also dabbled a bit in the thoroughbred game. My Father was truly my hero, and this book is certainly dedicated to his memory. My Father passed away suddenly on June 20th 2005. He was 83 years young.

But, over the better part of a 25-year period, he taught me almost everything there is to know about the care and training of any kind of racehorse. It was for about five of those 25 years, that I actually worked as a groom/2nd trainer. He also taught me almost everything I know about handicapping the races. He once said to me..."I can handicap a race better than guys can "fix" it!" I believed him then, and I think he has passed that trait onto me. What my Father meant by that statement was that having a horsemen's perspective on things is a totally invaluable asset to have, when handicapping a race. And, it is that (a Horsemen's perspective in/on handicapping horse races), I plan on giving to you the reader.

In writing this book, I've made a very concerted effort to try and incorporate as much pertinent horsemanship knowledge into many of the chapters, as a way to better serve the novice, average, or below average horseplayer. I truly believe that after reading this book, you will immediately come away with a better sense of yourself (as a horseplayer), and will soon realize where exactly it is you want to be as a horseplayer. You may come to the realization that you're always going to be just a recreational horseplayer, in the world of handicapping the races. Or, you might have a wonderful epiphany and realize that maybe you too can become a more successful horseplayer. Maybe, a "professional"!

When I first decided to start writing this, it was on the encouragement of many different family members, and my wonderful girlfriend Jenny Lynn. So, here it is and I hope it helps educate you a little more, so that your next experience at the track will also be a winning one.

Joseph J Tuttle

Chapter One
Not quite like your average book
(A brief history of The Racing Form)

{The Form}

The Daily Racing Form (as known simply as "The Form" to most of us) has been around since the late 1800's (1894 to be exact), as a publication. And, it truly has evolved just in my lifetime. But, as the old saying goes...."The more things change, the more they stay the same."

If memory serves me correctly, the origin of publication for The Daily Racing Form was in the little town of Hightstown, New Jersey.

I'd venture to guess that the most substantial change or revision done to the form over the last twenty-five years (or for its overall history as a publication for that matter) has been the addition of the "Beyer Speed Figures". The "Beyer Speed Figures" (which as I wrote about my disdain for, in my first book, "The Ultimate Guide To Handicapping The Horses"), have become a highly integral part of The Daily Racing Form.

His speed figures have helped sales, improved the form's validity (somewhat dramatically), since their inception, and have helped to spawn an almost "cult like" group of individuals known as "Beyer guys". These "Beyer guys" are individuals that strictly or solely base all of their selections on trends, patterns, and any other (what they might deem relevant) suggestive pieces of data directly from each horse's Beyer Speed Figures.

{Formulator 4.1}

The very first "Formulator" wasn't readily available to the general public until the late 90's (I do believe it was 1999), when www.drf2000.com first came about. Obviously, with it now being called Formulator 4.1 there have been many enhancements and improvements to the online racing form program, over the past nine years.

Formulator 4.1 is the most recent edition/version, which allows you the potential/future subscriber to construct The Racing Form, precisely as you would like to see it. And, it also includes many other invaluable features that simply just buying The Racing Form, does not afford to oneself. Quite obviously, in order to take full advantage of a product such as this, you're going to have to be relatively computer literate.

If you're not computer savvy (and the standard racing form is your only means of handicapping), then, you won't be left too far behind if you follow my teachings to the proverbial "T"!

I would strongly suggest to those of you who have purchased this book, to become computer literate ASAP, as a way to give yourself every opportunity to win.

Formulator 4.1 (in my humble opinion) would certainly be the most logical first step in helping to increase your chances of winning, on a more consistent basis.

As is the case in 99% of the books that you'll read in your life, you'll do so reading from left to right, and the racing form is no different. Or, is it? I will elaborate in great detail (as to the way in which I read The Racing Form), in the next chapter.

Chapter Two
How I read into things....
(Interpretation and Dissemination)

It's my contention that a lot of handicappers are a little on the lazy side. Especially those who like to "quick cap"! "Quick Capping" is an awful habit to develop. It typically occurs when an "Action Junkie" feels hurried to get a wager in, before a race is about to go off.

What is "Quick Capping" you might ask? "Quick Capping" was a practice that even I wasn't immune to, that I started noticing amongst me and my friends in the mid-90's. It is basically when; you just look at the midsection of the form on each horse, as a way to expedite the handicapping process. I NEVER do that anymore, nor should you!

But it does exist; it was truly like a plague for me and for most of my friends for a little spell there in the mid to late 90's. It's of the utmost importance to recognize and stay cognizant to when you might be falling into the trappings of "Quick Capping".

There will be an *index of terms* (placed in the back of this book), so that you will be able to better acquaint yourself with some of my vernacular.

Sorry for that little diatribe. Now, back on point!

{The "Beyer Speed Figures"}

By far and away, the most prevalent and/or talked about piece of suggestive data in The Racing Form, over the past fifteen years, would be the "Beyer Speed Figures". So, I might as well start there, even though it pains me to do so.

As I wrote about in my first book, I certainly do have an overwhelmingly antagonistic viewpoint on the "Beyer Speed Figures".

So, why do I have such an overwhelming bias against it?

It's my contention since Mr. Andrew Beyer is not God and/or omnipotent, and his formula suddenly gets placed in the hand(s) of many different person(s), at many different track(s) (which in my humble opinion dilutes the formula), that it simply becomes far too "subjective", at some point. This subjectivity factor of which I speak, has led me to believe that his numbers ARE NEVER 100% ACCURATE!

I do believe that it is the form that allows one to properly decipher and disseminate information quickly and accurately. And, I must admit that I do indeed use Mr. Beyer's speed figures, but only as a bit of a "barometer". The word "Barometer" that I used to describe the Beyer Speed Figures is the same way that I described my usage of his numbers, in my first book.

I will elaborate much more, (and in much greater detail); as to an actual formula that I'm going to share with you, in chapter 3 entitled "Knowing the numbers (Actual applied practices and theories)".

{The "Dates"}

As I've already mentioned, 99% of all books that you read, will be from left to right. Now, the form is virtually no different, except for in the way in which I'm going to teach you how to read it. I have devoted a chapter later on in this book (chapter 5 called Notes, the "Comment Line" lies and Videotape), which is to help teach you the value of just how significant I believe the comment line is.

And, just how much I believe most handicappers neglect it, was my primary reasoning for deciding to devote a chapter solely to the comment line. When I'm reading the form, the very first thing I look at is the time that has elapsed between races for every given horse, in every given race.

Then, the second piece of information that interests me the most is "The Comment Line".

An astonishing 81% of all horse's that win, fall into the following category; said horse's with 29 to 119 days off (from their last start, and assuming that at least one-third of the field do not meet this criteria), are the horse's that win just better than 4 out of every 5 races run, over the past 5 years! So, the first thing that I like to do is circle which horses meet those criteria. Now, in some cases (typically at your upper echelon meetings, such as Belmont, Saratoga, Santa Anita, etc.), you might be looking at an 8-horse field, in which every horse meets that criterion. So then what, you might ask?

Well, when I see that (but it truly is a rarity), I'm actually quite impressed by it because it suggests to me that every trainer that has a horse in said race has his or her horse "on track" (no pun intended).

Now, when I use the phrase "on track" I'm referring to the fact that it would seem that things are "on schedule" as prescribed by the trainer(s), for each horse in the race.

For the 29 to 119 days off "angle" I allocate a zero objectivity or subjectivity tolerance policy.

Meaning, if a horse is going off the 8–5 favorite in a particular race and he/she has only had two weeks off since its last start, and the 3-1 second choice has had 51 days off (since his/her last start), I will almost always, undoubtedly, side with the horse that has had the greater amount of time off.

The reason being, something my Father taught me long ago (whom I thought was an exceptional horseman)..."Less is more" and "More is better".

Obviously, a horse that is coming back after only two weeks rest, one can assume might be a little more stressed, than a horse having 51 days off. It's this kind of basic horsemanship knowledge/logic that can only help one become a better handicapper after being taught or subjected to such philosophies.

I briefly mentioned that every so often you will come across a race where every horse in said race has had 29 or more days off from his or her last start. Typically, those races are what are known as "stakes races".

A "stakes race" of any caliber, usually goes for a purse of $50,000 or more (although at some of your upper echelon race meetings "allowance races" can go for $50,000 to $60,000), and it's in these races that you will typically find the 29 to 119 angle most prevalent.

So Mr. Tuttle, what if a horse has had 120 or more days off?

Personally, unless the horse is on a 3 or more win streak, and is not moving up in class considerably, or has shown previously (in his or her past performance lines) the ability to race well with 120 or more days off, then I will not discount said horse immediately.

But, if we're talking about a cheap claiming race at Calder (or any other lower echelon race track venue for that matter), I will ultimately eliminate such a horse from consideration of winning said race, immediately.

This initial process/practice, especially in cheaper class races (such as claiming races); can really help expedite the handicapping process. It was devised as a way to help eliminate horses through process of elimination. The only time that this "angle" consistently loses, is when there are many Kentucky Derby horse's entered in The Preakness Stake, some two weeks later. You can count the number of Preakness winners on one hand, which won that race after skipping the Kentucky Derby, over the past twenty-five years.

{Class Characteristics}

"Switching Leads" From a horsemen's or a gambler's perspective, "switching leads" (and looking for whether or not a horse switches leads), is crucial. It basically acts as a "tell" on whether or not a horse may have any degree of professionalism, class, or stamina.

One of the main characteristics a horse with any amount of "class" will show, on a consistent basis, is the ability to "Switch Leads" at the top of the stretch.

"Switching Leads" is actually something that about 90% of racehorses instinctively know how to do.

But, it can also be a true sign of class (as to the manner in which they're doing it), and this is the primary reason why I believe that it is indeed a "sign of class".

A horse that doesn't "switch leads" typically is either sore or poorly trained. Especially, if it's a trait that he or she always possesses on a race-by-race basis. If a horse doesn't "switch leads" on a consistent basis, one could deduce that said horse is lacking a little in the class department.

You should look for a horse to "switch leads" at either the top of the stretch, or at the very least at some point during the stretch.

Now what exactly does "switching leads" mean? "Switching leads", is when a horse goes from his/her left lead to their right lead out of necessity, due to the left side being fatigued from running seventy-five percent of the race on his or her left lead. Although, I can think of one horse that had a hard time switching over, and was an extremely classy individual, his name was Alydar.

Now if memory serves me correctly, in all three of the Classic Races of 1978 (Kentucky Derby, Preakness, and Belmont Stakes), the great horse Alydar wound up losing all three races by a combined length and a half to Affirmed, because, he never once switched over to his right lead in any one of those three races. It does/can make a difference!

But, (and this is mainly in young horses), if a 2 or 3 yr-old horse looks sharp in victory, and doesn't "switch leads", it most likely means that the horse wants/needs more distance. That's the only time that a horse not "switching leads", is a good sign, in my professional opinion.

{Other Physical "Tells"}

Another trait that a horse with "class" will invariably show on a fairly regular basis is with the ears. Yes, I said the ears! If a horse is getting the saddle placed on his/her back (in the paddock), and the horse's ears are sticking straight up/out (at attention), then, that is a pretty classy individual. It is a trait that suggests that said horse is extremely "sharp" and ready to race (as in the horse cannot wait to get in the gate), and it is typically a great sign right before said horse goes to the track!

"White Socks"

A lot of old time horsemen (especially Quarter Horse trainer's), will say that a horse with "four white socks, is no good!" "Four white socks" is a direct reference to any horse having white legs from the knee to the ankle. A lot of old-timer's believe that a horse that possesses this trait will eventually go lame.

I personally, do not subscribe to that logic at all and neither should you. Although, if I find myself looking at a dozen two year-olds being prepared for a race in the paddock somewhere, I'd rather see just "two white socks" instead of four, and I'd much rather see them on the hind legs!

It may hold water with younger horses (as this has a bit more truth to it with two year-olds), but if you find yourself down at the paddock looking at a bunch of older horses, (in a cheap claiming race), then, I wouldn't let this enter any part of your thinking, as it pertains to handicapping.

"Blazes and Stars"

I'd venture a guess that about 70% of racehorses have either a small "star" on their forehead, or a "blaze". My Father was a big believer that a horse with a "very well-defined blaze" was a horse that would show/have a lot of front-running speed. Over the years this was certainly a trait that my Father brought to my attention on many occasions.

A lot of well-respected horsemen also believe there is a large bit of truth behind the "well-defined blaze".

So, what is exactly is meant by a "well-defined blaze", you might ask?

A horse with this "well-defined blaze" trait usually is born with it. It typically starts at the eyes (centered right between the eyes), and runs straight down to the beginning of the horse's nose, and/or in some cases it bleeds into and becomes a part of that particular horse's nose. There has been many a Kentucky Derby Winner to possess one of those two traits. It is a welcomed and useful handicapping tool, (primarily amongst young horses), and probably will be until the end of time.

Since 1988 (which was the last time a Filly won the Kentucky Derby named Winning Colors); there have been a total of 21 Kentucky Derby races run, and in that time there have been 14 winners to have a "blaze" or a "star" on their face.

{The Comment Line}

I've established the first thing one should look for are the "dates" (located on the far left of the Racing Form), in which each horse last raced. Along with the actual amount of days rested since said horse's last start. I believe the second most important part of the form to look over, is to the far right..."The Comment Line".

The Comment Line is the most pertinent piece of data in that part of the form, besides the last variable listed, which is the number of horses that he/she raced against in said horse's last start.

Now, the reason why I put such a high degree of importance on the "Comment Lines" is due to the fact it gives you a wonderful gauge as to what type of company a horse has been keeping.

That, in and of itself I find to be an extremely important piece of suggestive data that must be evaluated, on a horse-by-horse basis.

Only after one has the ability to "gauge" or determine the "class" variant of any given horse, can one quickly and without peril, disregard certain horses from serious consideration. This practice does take a bit of actual time to develop. But, after one has watched as many races as I have, it becomes almost second nature in determining the "class level" of any given horse.

I must admit that I've cultivated my ability to gauge a horse's "class" through a lot of videotape analysis. This is a practice that I've talked about at length in my first book: "The Ultimate Guide to Handicapping the Horses".

I believe that through videotape analysis one can make extremely accurate judgments on each and every horse viewed. A wonderful example of what I'm talking about as far as being able to eliminate certain horses from serious consideration is by just employing a little common sense.

If you're looking at the past performances of a certain horse, and the horse consistently shows an unwillingness to *pass* other horses (as in gets away 4th, drops back to 6th by the second call, and then winds up coming in 5th), then I don't consider that "passing horses". Technically, yes, the horse did pass one through the stretch. But, that could have just been a "tired one". And, if it were a 10 or 11-horse race then this is a horse that really didn't show me much of anything, especially, not any real/high degree of "class", in my humble opinion. "Classy horse(s)" typically show a willingness to pass on a consistent basis.

Any diehard baseball fan has heard of Bill James, and has also heard of Sabermetrics. A baseball player is an athlete, correct? Well, racehorses are athletes too. So I've adopted the basic premise of how one derives on-base percentage with a baseball player, to horse racing.

You simply count up the total number of horses that said horse has raced against (throughout however many past performance lines that DRF allots for that particular horse), divide that number by the total number of races shown, and you're left with an average amount of horse's that "said horse" has raced against. Then, you simply count the total number of horses that "said horse" has beaten (line by line in the past performances), and/or "passed".

I personally, like to go by horses "passed" instead of horses beaten.

Now, in the event that you're dealing with a "stone cold front runner", it seems painfully obvious to me that you then need to employ the tactic of horses "beaten", rather than horses "passed", with that particular brand of racehorse.

Now that I've just shown you a few highly sophisticated ways to determine class and ability, I do believe you're ready for the next step, which is chapter three.

Chapter Three
Knowing the numbers
(Actual applied practices and theories)

In the previous chapter I talked about my three most pertinent sections of the form that I look over before I start "doing up" any numbers. In this chapter, that is all I'm going to talk about, and the way in which I come up with specific number types to support and/or make a case for any given horse, in any given race.

A very long time ago, when I first started to fall in love with mathematics, within the realm of horse racing (I guess I was about 16 or 17 at the time), I devised a "universal number" (that I applied as a universal track variant number), for each horse in every race.

This was long before the Beyer Speed Figures were published in the Daily Racing Form. But, even after the Beyer Speed Figures began to emerge as a force in handicapping, I was still holding my own with my "universal number theory". Once I realized there was some validity to Mr. Beyer's numbers, I incorporated those numbers into my already unique system.

So what is the universal variant number? First off, when you're looking at any particular horse in the DRF, immediately to the right of the odds in which the horse went off at last time out, you'll see a speed rating number and a track variant number. Now, unless two horses are coming out of the same exact race on the same exact day, at the same exact track obviously, the variant number always seems to be different from horse to horse, and race to race.

So at the ripe old age of 16, I decided that I would give a "universal number" (20) as a variant for every horse. If the DRF says a horse last raced on a (14) variant racetrack last time out, I automatically raise it to 20, and then subtract 6 points from the DRF speed rating. If I'm looking at a different horse, and said horse raced on a (27) variant racetrack, then naturally I would add (instead of subtract), 7 points to that horse's speed rating. It's my contention that by doing this you incorporate a lot more mathematics, and a lot less subjectivity, to the numbers, that the DRF provides to the gambler's on a daily basis.

It wasn't until the mid 90's, and about 3 or 4 years into the "Beyer Speed Figures" being published in the DRF that I decided to add this derivative to my system. What I incorporated (into my already somewhat successful system), by using the Beyer Speed Figures, was an added element that began to produce an even higher percentage of accurate selections.

So much so, that I can now gauge approximately how many lengths one horse should beat another horse by in any given race, and soon so will you.

Here is how it's done...

By utilizing my "universal variant number", you're then able to derive a more accurate DRF speed rating, and then you simply add that number to the Beyer Speed Figure number, and divide by 2. Now there are some instances where the racing form will show a dash (--) where the track variant number should be. In these instances, simply use the next race available in that horse's past performance lines.

This new method of deriving speed ratings for each horse will indeed produce more winners for you. Now the way in which you can deduce how many lengths one horse is better than another (in theory), is, what I call "The 5-point rule".

The 5-point rule simply means for every 5 points one horse has a higher speed rating than another that equals one length.

In the event you're involved in handicapping a race whereby the horse with the top number has an (85), and the second highest numbered horse has a number of (81), then, in my humble opinion a high degree of discretion needs to be invoked.

Example:

If the horse with the (81) number has a few added intangibles in his or her favor, over the horse with the (85) number (such as better jockey, better post, and/or first or second time Lasix), then quite obviously these are concessions that need to be considered, and quite possibly the horse with the lower number may actually be the better horse to wager on.

It's this type of "discretion" that you need to take full responsibility for, at all times. When it comes to actually interpreting the numbers, you need to make sure of two things; A) that your figures are correct (it's always good to stay disciplined to the practice of double checking) and B) more importantly, I found it extremely helpful (I think you will too), to devise your own grading system for other intangibles.

Example:

You're involved in handicapping a race where there are eight total horses in said race. Two horses have identical top numbers, and three out of the remaining six are within 5 points of those top two. Then what? Now as I've already prefaced, if a horse is within 5 points of another, that is the equivalent to only one length.

So, I've deemed it very necessary to devise a grading system for some of the other "outside intangibles" (such as a positive jockey change from a horse's last race, a significant drop in class, or first time in a new barn) that are made readily available in the racing form at all times. It seemed very obvious to me many years ago, that some kind of grading system was going to be necessary for these types of highly contentious races. With the situation like in the above-mentioned paragraph, I would first try to differentiate the top two horses by intentionally creating some possible separation through a points scale system for some of these "other intangibles".

So if horse A has an (85) number, and horse B has the same, but horse A is getting a big jockey improvement and horse B is retaining the same jockey from his or her last race, then naturally it stands to reason that horse A deserves some added points for this jockey improvement.

I usually add an additional 2 points for a horse in this situation. So now, horse A is no longer an (85), but an (87). Now, in the event that one of the 80-numbered horse's (of those mythical three that were tied with an (80) speed rating), were to have three or four other intangibles that might improve their overall speed rating/score, then, that horse would now garner a number somewhere between (86) to (88).

I typically delegate 2 points for each outside intangible that I deem necessary to improve a horse's overall speed rating/score, if indeed it is deserving of it. Now, a horse such as this would be very forwardly placed in my handicapping thoughts, as a possible candidate for the win. But, only if at least three "outside intangibles" improve this horse's overall score, from an (80) to at least an (86).

Again, a lot of the onus falls on you to make these very discretionary calls. As I've said once before in one of my other books, "This book is your vessel and I am no more than its Captain. You, are on your way to becoming your own Captain". When I said that, I meant it quite literally. The responsibility that one must undertake in making these "discretionary calls" falls squarely on your shoulders. Just a little food for thought when you start handicapping "The Tuttle Way".

*****Since I'm not employed by DRF or their parent company, I am restricted as to the type of example (below), that I'm about to show you on the next few pages.*****

(Below is the basic feel of the last charted line, of a mythical horse, that you might see in the Daily Racing Form, on a regular dirt surface.)

4 Jeneration

11apr08 6Del fst 6f :22 :46 :59 1:12 Md25000 **61** 1 2 35 1
1 25 Johnson JJ

(The above-mentioned line is basically the first half (or left side),
of any horse's charted line in the DRF, and a brief description of
what you'd see from the far left, to the middle of the page.)
11apr08; refers to the date that this mythical horse last
raced.

6Del; this refers to the actual race number, and the actual
track venue (in this case 6Del refers to the 6th race @
Delaware Park).

fst; this refers to that day's track condition (**fst** stands for
fast, **sly** stands for sloppy, **my** stands for muddy and **wf**
stands for wet/fast).

6f; this quite obviously refers to the distance that this horse
last raced at. (6f is simply short for **six furlongs**)

:22 :46 :59 1:12; these numbers are what's know as the
"fractional times", or as more advanced handicappers refer
to them as **"The internal fractions"**.

:22 - the time that the horse leading at that marker
went/ran (in seconds), **This number is also referred to as
the "first call"** (I will elaborate more on "the first call" in a
moment).

:46 - this number refers to the "second call", and again,
this number refers to the time of the actual horse leading,
at the **"second call"**.
:59 - this number refers to the time of the actual horse
leading at this particular call, which is known as the **"deep
stretch call"**. (The **"deep stretch call"** is almost always the
point of call with only one furlong remaining in said race).

1:12 - this quite obviously is the winner's **final time**. (In the case of our mythical horse **Jeneration,** she went one full second slower, due to the fact that she came in second, and lost by 5 lengths). **1/5ᵗʰ of a second is equivalent to every length beaten**, so if the winner went **1:12**, and she lost by **5 lengths**, then she obviously went her final time in **1:13**.

Md25000; refers to the "class" or classification restrictions of said race. [In this case or instance, **Md25000** means that the race was **restricted to "Maidens"** with a **claiming price** attached on them of **25,000.00**.] This means that if an owner wanted to have our mythical horse, said owner could do so simply by "putting in a claim" on this horse, prior to the start of the race. **This is the norm in the world of "claiming races"**.

61; this **"bold" number of (61)** is our mythical horse's last race **"Beyer Speed Figure"**.

1 2 35 1 1 25 - this group of numbers are (from left to right).... (1) Our horse broke from post position number one. Then, (2) is what is commonly referred to as **"the break"**, call. **35 The (3) with the small (5) next to it,** refers to the actual position of our horse @ **"the first call"**, and the exact distance (**in lengths**), that our horse was running behind the leader. The number (1), immediately after the (3) refers to the horse's position at **"the second call".** The next number (1), refers to **"the deep stretch call"**. Finally, the number (2) with the small (5) at the end refers to our horse's finishing position at the wire and the number of lengths the eventual winner beat our mythical horse by.

Johnson JJ; this refers to the Jockey that rode said horse for that particular race.

Next, I will explain the right side of the form (as it pertains to my own personal rating/grading systems), and give you, the reader, some added sights into "The Tuttle Way" of handicapping the races.

Right side of form continuation...

Directly to the "right" of the name of the Jockey, is what I consider the right side of the form. The first item worth mentioning (to the right of the Jockey's name), is the **"medication line"**. The **"medication line"** is typically placed right next to the **"weight line"**. Directly attached to the "weight line" is the "equipment line" [a horse showing a lower case "b" next to their previously assigned weight, was wearing "blinkers"], and that is an extremely pertinent piece of information. The **"weight line"** precedes the actual **"off odds"** line. The "off odds" are based on a 1.00 scale [If you see a horse that went off at odds of **16.60**], this means that if said horse would have won, or did win, it would have paid 16.60 per dollar wagered on it, plus your initial 2.00 bet, back. **So, on a two-dollar wager, said horse would have paid a return of 35.20 total for 2.00 wagered.**

Johnson   JJ   L120b   16.60   74-17   Whirly1205   Jeneration1203 comtwopapa1191 tired late 8

L120b; this bit of information is relative to three actual pieces of data, in one

"L"= Lasix user. **120**, is the weight that said horse carried in its last race, and the **"b"**; means that said horse wore **"blinkers"** in its **last race**.

16.60; are the odds that said horse went off at post time, on a 1.00 scale.

74-17; the **(74) number is the speed rating** given to said horse, and the (17) was that day's **"track variant"**.

{Now, using my method of generating a more accurate speed rating from these published numbers, the (17) turns into a (20) (the number (20) being my "universal variant" number), would in-turn, would "Lower" the (74) number to a slightly lower number of (71).

Then, I take the (71) and simply add it to the "Beyer Speed Figure" number (which was 61), which would give me a combined total of (132), which I then divide by 2, which equals (66) as the new and more accurate speed rating.}

Whirly 1205 Jeneration 1203 Comtwopapa 1191 tired late 8

Finally, directly above is what's known as the "competition line", along with the "comment line" (in this case says "tired late"), and lastly the number of horse's that was in said race.

After the name of the horse you'll see the weight that the horse carried, along with a slightly smaller number. The slightly smaller number is the amount of lengths that said horse beat his or her next nearest competitor.

The final two pieces of information that are in any horse's last charted line in the racing form, is the "comment line" (in this case our mythical horse has a comment line of "tired late"), and the final piece of information, as I've already mentioned, is the total number of horses (including the mythical horse), that were in said race.

I briefly spoke earlier about a Mr. Bill James who is the creator of Sabermetrics. *{which is what Fantasy baseball players and even actual General Manager's use as a barometer for actual talent/ability of prospects}*

I guess it was about the early-90's when I remember sportscaster Bob Costas giving his ringing endorsement towards the validity of "Sabermetrics", and Mr. Bill James. It was at this point that I had an epiphany, and realized that some of the same principals could be used in handicapping and evaluating the actual talent/ability level(s) of racehorses.

Just as Mr. James calculates total bases accumulated, divided by plate appearances, as a way to determine OBP (on base percentage), I've applied the same logic to any given horserace. Especially with maiden races, I feel that there is a lot of validity in the way in which I use it.

I briefly mentioned earlier, that I employ this logic by adding the total number of horses "passed" (on a race by race basis); by the total number of competitor's faced. This "system", usually derives a percentage that can be used as a gauge, in comparing one horse to another.

I also feel it is an above average way to determine "class", by commingling that number to said horse's average earning per start. The two uniquely different percentages can be very telling, if you know what you're looking at.

Example:

If a horse has had only five lifetime starts, and has been involved in only eight horse fields (and has come from dead last in all of his starts), in winning 4 of 5 starts, and was 6th in the lone one "bad effort", then, what is this horse's "passing percentage"?
(5) Lifetime start x (7) other competitor's per start would equal (35) total rivals faced. (4) Wins (in which said horse came from dead last to win all four), would equal (28) passed horses. Plus, our mythical horse had one "bad start" (in which he only passed two), would now come to total of (30) horses passed, out of a maximum of (35) in all, would equal a "passing percentage of 86%.

Now, it's my contention that a truly "classy" individual (more so in the early stages of a horse's career) should average approximately $1,000.00 per horse "passed", in overall earnings (for about the first 5 or 6 starts).

*****If a horse shows no "stake race" lines, and/or "allowance" lines, and is currently racing in claiming races (and is 5 yrs-old or older), then, I'd cut that average amount (per horse passed), in half, to $500 per horse passed, and just for that current year. For it would be impossible to go by lifetime earnings in all likelihood. *****

Obviously with horse's that show nothing but grade 1, grade 2, or grade 3 races on their card, I employ as a rule of thumb of $10,000 in earnings per horse passed. And, in your supreme upper echelon stakes events (such as the Kentucky Derby, The Preakness, etc., where every horse shows nothing but grade 1's, and a few grade 2's, then I assume a higher measure (that I also deem to be more accurate), of $30,000 in earnings per horse passed, in a given year.

Obviously, if a horse has only made 11 lifetime starts and is involved in one of these types of races, then, you would most certainly take that into consideration, and go by lifetime earnings instead of yearly.

In the case of our mythical horse (especially with an 86% percentile of passing other horses), I would hope to see a little more than just 30k on this particular horse's card, as far as lifetime earnings are concerned. If there were less than $30,000 in lifetime earnings (through those five starts) of said horse, one could automatically put into question that horse's "competition" level that said horse has previously faced as being relatively suspect. Wouldn't you agree? In closing out this chapter and at the risk of sounding redundant, I feel the need to preface once more the fact that all of these new "interpretive techniques" (that I'm willing to share to you) have to be handled with the utmost discretion.

The greatest part of handicapping the races (at least in my humble opinion) is the fact that all of us are going to have varying opinions, on a race-by-race basis, and therein lies the beauty of it.

Chapter Four
Understanding the "Internal Fractions"

If you've ever watched a cycling race on TV, then you've probably noticed (on more than one occasion), that every so often a cyclist will "break from the pack", open-up on the rest of the field, and try to "steal" the race by getting the jump on his competitor's. In the world of horse racing this is what is commonly known as "Bottoming–out the field". The prevailing logic behind this strategy is to make it as hard as possible for the other competitor's to "catch-up".

In the process, it can force the hand of a few of those competitor's to "use their horse" (as in expending energy), sooner then originally anticipated.

So, what does this have to do with understanding "internal fractions, you might ask? Everything and nothing, allow me to elaborate. Here's a shinning example of a race that I was involved with (from a handicapping perspective), just recently. It was a completely pace-less race in which there were absolutely no "front runners", or any "deep closers".

So, I remembered one of these "plodder" types (a "plodder" is a horse that consistently runs "mid-pack" with no real "early speed") once was a "front runner" (when he was a 2 yr-old), and with my trainer's cap on, I said to myself... "If this guy were to get hustled out of the gate, he could easily go a 23 flat opening quarter and build a 4 or 5 length lead, maybe get "brave" on the front-end, and never look back!"

Well, that's exactly what happened and I scored to the tune of a $15.00 mutual for a $2.00 bet. I had $100.00 to win on him (that returned a profit of $650.00), and I wound up hitting a $1638.00 pick-3.

Enough of my trip down memory lane, and now on to the meat and potatoes of understanding the meaningfulness behind the "internal fractions". The internal fractions (otherwise known as the "quarterly splits"), have been called so (as a euphemism), only since about the year 2000 that I can remember.

I remember reading a stat in the early 90's that; 80% of horse's that go on to win, "are within 5 lengths of the leader, or on the lead, at the top of the stretch. Now that stat I remember reading many years ago, probably is just as true or accurate now, in the year 2008.

I still find myself "trip handicapping" (I will get into the definition of "trip handicapping" later on, or you can just check the index), with a more than 15 year old stat floating around in my head at all times, primarily because I still find a lot of truth in it.

Here is a scenario that I'm sure you're going to encounter time and time again, especially if you're wagering on some of the upper echelon racetracks in the country. It's a 6-furlong sprint race, and there are 2 or 3 "speed horses" or "front runners" in the race. So, how does one determine which horse is going to actually be in front before they hit the first turn, and will that horse get put under some pressure by one of the other "front runners"?

Well to properly answer that last question, you need to ask yourself one very simple question. Out of these two or three "front runners", which one has the most advantageous post? Now just because one of these 3 front-runners has the rail, does not necessarily mean that horse has the most advantageous post. Quite the contrary, it's the horse that has the 7 or 8 post (if it's a 7 or 8 horse field), that has the true tactical advantage.

Now, let's say all 3 "front runners" show in their past performances the ability to run an opening quarter mile in 22 seconds flat. Again, how do you determine which horse or horse's are going to be out in front early on? It's always been my belief (and the belief of literally thousands of horsemen world wide), that the "front runner" with the outside post has a tactical advantage.

Having the ability to "flank" one or both of the other "front runners", is not only tactically advantageous, but, in doing so the jockey can avoid the stupidity of a 3-horse speed duel. And, the jockey is giving his horse a clear target to run at, to "lock on" to the one or two horses inside of his horse, turning for home. This is all any trainer and/or owner can ask of a jockey to do for his or her horse (from a positioning standpoint), of that point in the race.

Another crucial factor to consider (that 99% of handicappers do not) is that of "centrifugal force". Now, I'm not trying to turn handicapping horse racing into rocket science, but a variable such as centrifugal force needs to be taken into account.

Have you ever wondered why so many "horses on the outside" win photos? It's because of centrifugal force. It's the jockey/horse from their extreme outside post position that can use centrifugal force to their advantage. They do so, by "sling shotting" off of the final turn, after flanking the other speed horse or speed horses for the first two thirds of the race. This is much more noticeable to the naked eye in harness racing, than it is in thoroughbred racing, yet it still exists.

{Speed in Theory}

What does it really mean when a horse goes a 22 flat opening quarter? Well, if it's a one-mile race, it means that horse just traveled a quarter of a mile in 22 seconds, which means if he kept that pace up for the next three quarters, he would cover the mile in 1:28. Now as we all know, that is theoretically impossible.

The fastest of milers (in the United States or in the world for that matter), can only cover a flat mile in about 1:32 or 1:33. Which means, that over the next three-quarter's (or six furlongs), the fastest of milers is going to incrementally go slower due to natural variables that exist within any distance race. Variables such as the turn(s), the field size, and fatigue, will inevitably cause this inability to cover a mile in 1:28 flat.

Now by no means am I suggesting that 1:33 (for a flat mile is a bad and/or slow time), because I know full well that it's quite fast, and so should you.

The primary reason why we're never going to see a flat mile covered in the low or high 120's is because of the old saying "pace makes the race".

A wonderful example of what I'm talking about is when a "sprinter" enters a stakes race at a route of ground (a "route of ground" is also known as a race around two turns), and this "sprinter" (who has never shown the ability to win at a "route of ground" or further), is simply in the race to act as a "rabbit". This "rabbit"; that inevitably gets passed like he's tied to a post by the time they reach the top of the stretch, has already ensured a very fast pace in the earlier stages of the race. But, even for horses that are finishing with a flourish down the stretch, a level of fatigue has set in from "getting into position", truly does ensure the fact that we'll never see a flat mile in the low to high 120's, ever!

And, in the next section of this chapter, I will elaborate as to why; along with discussing something I like to call "Fractional Interpretation".

I'm willing to concede that I'm probably not the first handicapper to interpret the fractions in the manner in which I do.

{Fractional Interpretation}

Example:

Hypothetically, if you're about to place a wager on a horse that consistently is about five or six lengths behind at the "first call" of the opening quarter mile of the races that he's involved in (which are of the 6 furlong variety), and the leaders are consistently going in 21.4 to 22.1 (of that opening quarter mile in said races), then it is safe to assume that said horse does not posses the ability to go an opening quarter mile faster than about 23 seconds flat.

Now let's say this mythical horse that you're about to place a wager on found himself on the lead at the "second call", of that 6 furlong race (the second call in a 6 furlong race would be the half, or at the "quarter pole"); which would be the top of the stretch. Let's assume the half went in 45 seconds flat. That means that said horse went a faster next 2 furlongs then he went his opening 2 furlongs. This means, that his opening quarter was 23 flat and his second quarter went in 22 seconds flat. Now with all this being said, what would you consider a good final 2 furlongs, and a good final time?

In the year 2008, a relatively fast 6-furlong final time is about 1:10 flat. So, in the case of our mythical horse above, he went his last 2 furlongs in 25 seconds flat.

Obviously, if he would have gone in 1:08 flat, I would be incredibly impressed, due to the fact that once said horse started his brush towards the lead; he would have only slowed down by one second instead of three.

This is also how you can determine how strong of a "brush" a horse might have, which can ultimately lead to more winners and a better overall opinion (for yourself to develop), of horseflesh.

{What I like to do looks something like this...}

:22 (for the horse that led after the opening quarter)
:23 *(my "horse of interest" was sitting 3rd, 5 lengths off the leader)*

:45(the time that the leader of said race hit the half at)
:45.1 *(my horse was still sitting 3rd, but now only one length off the lead)*

At this point you need to calculate *three* of four highly intrinsic variables:

A. How fast did my horse go from the "first call" to the "second call"? (In this case, the answer would be: (:22.1).

B. Did my horse run a faster "second call" than the leader ran his "second call"? In this case the answer is: "Yes", (:22.1) compared to (:23).

C. Did my horse run a faster "second call" than the leader's "first call"? In this case the answer is: "No", (:22.1) compared to (:22 flat).

The *fourth variable* is an excellent way to "rate" (no pun intended), horses on an individualized "horse vs. horse" basis. This final variable consists of simple addition/subtraction of the fractional times, to be used as a barometer, as a way to further develop your overall handicapping abilities.

{The *fourth variable*}
Proper "Interpretation" of fractions

So far, through the first two calls and two of the previous three "variable questions", my horse or "*horse of interest*" hasn't actually outworked this mythical lead horse for the first four furlongs (even though he is only one length behind), as they're about to go headlong down the stretch, and he was 5 lengths behind after the opening quarter of the race.

How can/did I make such an assertion?

It really is some very rudimentary mathematics. First off, said horse was 5 lengths behind at the "first call", and only one length off at the "second call". This would indicate that said horse went $4/5_{ths}$ (or four lengths), faster, from point of call to the next point of call.

But, remember, my *"horse of interest"* went a 23 second opening quarter, as compared to the lead horse who went in 22 (that is one whole second faster), and *one whole second* is approximately $1/5^{th}$ of a second faster, than the $4/5_{ths}$ that my *"horse of interest"* outran the lead horse during that "second call".

The previous two paragraphs are the primary reason why a lot of "speed handicappers" or "trip handicappers" wind-up broke most days. They're simply misinterpreting the fractions as compared to the ways of my teachings.

Determining which horse is "doing the better work", typically doesn't lie in the final part of a race, but in the first two parts of a race. This is a brand of logic and a methodology not shared by most, and *most* lose! So, keep that in mind!

Another one of my highly useful techniques that I love to use I call the TCB (Tuttle Class Barometer), and here is how it works. You simply add up the total number of starts made by the field, and divide that number by the total number of wins garnered by those participants.

Example:

A cheap field of 6,250 claimers at Calder would have a likely "Operative Number" of 70. The "Operative Number" of (70), is the current average speed rating for this particular class of racehorse. In this mythical field of racehorses, they might have 104 starts and 20 total wins, and you'll be left with a number like 19% as that field's overall win percentage. Then, you subtract the win-percentage number (19) from (70) which leaves you with an "Optimal Number" of (51).

After these calculations are done, you simply go through the racing form, horse by horse, and circle every number of (51) or higher. The horse garnering the highest amount of Beyer speed ratings (at 51 or over) in that particular event, would likely be the most logical horse to place a win bet on.

I must admit that these applied methodologies and practices are much more useful in smaller-sized field races, or in upper echelon stakes events. This is definitely another little tidbit to keep in mind, as you begin to navigate the form via "The Tuttle Way".

Chapter Five
Notes, the "Comment Line" lies and Videotape

In this chapter I'm going to help you explore the wonderful world of videotape analysis, as it truly does apply to handicapping the races. And, I plan to regurgitate a lot of what I spoke about in my first book, along with some additional thoughts (as to why the "Comment Lines" in the DRF are sometimes highly inaccurate), and on how we as Gambler's have a real/fundamental "informational advantage" over "The House", in this the year 2008.

In the last part of the previous paragraph I stated that I believe…"We as Gambler's have a real/fundamental "informational advantage" over "The House", in this the year 2008."

Well, in the next chapter entitled "Betting from Home", I plan to elaborate much more on that statement. But for now let's tackle the two topics at hand.

{Videotape Note Taking Practices}

When utilizing race replays you should always bear in mind that you may find a diamond in the rough. It helps to have an open mind. *"It's absolutely crucial to break yourself of the bad habit of only looking at the horse you've wagered on, when watching a race, or race replays."*

You may see something that a jockey and/or horse did in a race that you weren't even prepared to see. Whatever it is you might see needs to go into a physical notebook.

The notebook needs to be quite site specific. The date, weather conditions at the time of the race (if pertinent), class of the race, time of the race, if unusually fast or slow, (this should be something that is common knowledge to you, whether or not a race is unusually fast or slow for a particular class of horse), and finally, whether or not the horse you're watching "switched leads" down the stretch.

Another important note taking practice (in determining just how "strong" any particular race is), would be to divide the number of lengths that the winner ended-up beating the last place horse by (in lengths), by the number of horses in said race.

Example:

If the winner of a particular race wins by twenty-seven lengths over the last place horse in the race, and it was a nine horse field, then the number derived is a (3).

A "derived number" of (3) or less is considered an average or slightly above average performance. A number of (4 or 5) is obviously a little bit better effort and a number of (6) or higher is superb.

I also believe that this practice can help immensely in conjunction with determining validity to the Beyer speed figures listed in the Daily Racing Form. Here's a shining example of what I'm talking about. Let's say you just watched a horse win with a "derived number" of (6).

If the Beyer's speed figure (which is incredibly subjective I might add), doesn't amount to an (85) or more, the next time you see the form on that horse, you may be able to find some hidden value on that particular horse. If the Beyer number ends up at (86) or higher, then, you'll know that it is a fairly accurate speed figure, and the betting value of that particular horse may not be very good.

And just for the record, if a horse ends up with a "derived number" of (6) or higher, chances are it was a pretty dominant performance to begin with. Basically, it means that if a horse earned a number of (6), and it was a seven-horse field, the winning horse must have beaten the 7th place horse by 42 lengths!

{The Comment Line}......Does it lie???

Are the "Comment Lines" accurate, and/or do they lie? Well, I'll let you decide. I'm going to show you what is on my newest website venture (www.findthetroublehorse.com), and an excerpt from my first book..."The Ultimate Guide To Handicapping The Horses: From a Horseman and a Gambler".

Straight from www.findthetroublehorse.com

I recently wagered on a horse named Caressive (on Thanksgiving Day 2007 in Hollywood Park's second race), in which this horse had a Beyer number of only (59).

It was the 6ᵗʰ worst Beyer number (from all of the competitor's last start), of an eight-horse field. A totally impossible horse to play, if you are a "Beyer Guy"!

Besides the fact that I knew the horse was better than the number given, and I will expound upon that in a minute, I also knew that the "comment line" given was highly inaccurate. So, after scoping things out from the night before, I was salivating to say the least! That horse did indeed go on to win, and paid a hefty $15.00 for every two wagered.

I personally played her as a "key" (in exotic wagers), and I wagered $200.00 on her to win. The exotic wager was that day's early pick-4 (which I did go on to hit), and it paid $1,478.00. The two hundred dollar win bet yielded a profit of another $1,300.00.

Now, I just mentioned that another reason why I was so high on that horse was due to the comment line being "highly inaccurate". I will elaborate more on that in the next chapter, in the section entitled "Determining Value". But for now, let me explain just how I knew that the number (59 Beyer Speed Figure), given to that particular horse wasn't very accurate.

As I've mentioned already in great detail, the first thing I do in handicapping any race, is to look-up the video replay of each horse's last start. In said start of "Caressive" (1st race on October 25th @ Keeneland), she was almost definitely going to win, had she not been "checked hard" in between two rivals, with about 100 yards to go....(left in the race). Now, the official Racing Form version in the "comment line" read as follows: "4-5 wide, flattened out".

Don't believe it.....check it out?!

Excerpt from my first book...

"It mentioned nothing of what actually happened in the final 100 yards. Furthermore, it seems almost criminal for the "comment line" to be so unbelievably inaccurate. Just another shining example of why it's important to do your own investigating through video analysis. And, after doing said video analysis, I automatically gave her an additional 5 points. Then, after looking through the last races of the other competitor's, in that race, I was left unimpressed.

I determined that it might behoove me to allocate more time towards viewing that entire October 25th racing card at Keeneland that day (to see all of the "times" of the dirt races that day), in order to better determine whether or not "Caressive" was truly deserving of a number higher than the (64) I had her up to.

That is only part of the methodology that I employ, in making such a determination. After which, I calculate the overall average time per furlong run (for that day), in relation to the average seconds per furlong of the track record holder for each varying distance."

I'm assuming that most of the persons that write the charts for the form do not have much of a horsemanship background. Again, let us assume that I'm correct in my assumption. If so, then you must agree that rechecking the "comment line" through watching race replays is a must? The best example that my assumption might be correct is the fact that at least 30% of all racehorses (especially the younger ones), "climb" in the first quarter mile of a race. "Climbing"; in laymen's terms, is when a horse's front-end action is a little higher and quicker than it should be.

As a consequence of a horse that is "climbing", the horse may be expending a little too much energy in the early stages of a race, which in all likelihood can compromise that horse's chances of winning in the later stages of the race.

So, a "Comment Line" that you ALMOST NEVER SEE is something like the following... "Rank or Green early, climbing for opening ¼." Now, the only logical reason why a "comment line" such as that example is almost never shown must be due to the fact that the Daily Racing Form does NOT employ persons with a high degree of horsemanship knowledge. I don't find it irresponsible of them, just a slight oversight that probably needs to be rectified.

{Video Tape Analysis}

The true beauty in being a horseplayer in the year 2008 is the fact that there is an overabundance of information and websites such as mine that can only further and/or increase your chances for success.

Now I don't mean to break my arm patting myself on the back, but there is a page on my website (www.findthetroublehorse.com) called Recent Successes. On this page you'll find actual copy/pasting's of reminder e-mails from TVG.com, which I've simply uploaded on to my site.

Straight from www.findthetroublehorse.com....

Below are just a few of the recent winners provided by our service. And, if you have a TVG account, then, you'll know that you're looking at the actual "reminder emails", that they send out.

Dear Joseph,
Just a reminder:Fit Faze is scheduled to run on 5/1/2008 in Race 3 at Belmont. Don't forget to watch and wager at TVG.com   This guy paid a hefty 12-1!!!!

Dear Joseph,
Just a reminder:Harlene is scheduled to run on 4/27/2008 in Race 9 at Hollywood Park. Don't forget to watch and wager at TVG.com   HOW ABOUT A 33-1 (MAIDEN), IN A STAKES RACE!!!!

Dear Joseph,
Just a reminder:Powerofthepincus is scheduled to run on 4/21/2008 in Race 7 at Mountaineer. Don't forget to watch and wager at TVG.com This guy paid a hefty 26-1!!!!

Those three horse's alone, accounted for the vast majority of the profit that my clients and I made, for the month of April. On my website I offer that the horses that I give you (for the month), will hit the board on a 63% or better ratio. For the month of April my "troubled horses" hit the board exactly 70% (31 of 44), "Hit the Board". 17 were winners (with an overall average win price of $28.60) at an incredible 13-1 average ticket per $2.00 win payout!!!

Last I checked, 17 winners out of 44 horses is almost 40% (38.6 to be exact), and that alone with developing a keen eye, and an uncanny ability to properly utilize video tape analysis, is precisely what I'm talking about. I truly believe that anybody can hone this particular skill. Regardless of educational background, little or no horsemanship experience, or actual practical experience in the world of handicapping horses, in this manner.

I can say with a straight face that the person I was, and how I handicapped at age 24, compared to now is absolutely worlds apart. I believe the primary reason behind all of my successes, was due to the advent of the Internet. I steadfastly believe that one cannot fear technology (The Internet), AND EXPECT TO WIN, in the year 2008!

I hadn't planned on using this section of this chapter as a way to promote my site, but I just realized something; as I was writing that last paragraph. What better way for someone to learn "what to look for", then by revisiting my actual notations, of what I send out on a daily basis to my paying clients!

Here's an excerpt of an actual email sent to one of my clients, that has chosen The Meadowlands (as one of his three tracks per month), for my videotape analysis, through my website... www.findthetroublehorse.com

MEADOWLAND FOR 05/07/08

1-3......NTR (Nothing To Report)

4th.....#6 WESTERN BON BON- 1ST TIME KNEE SPREADERS, AND SHE TOOK A NEW LIFE MARK......NEXT OUT, THEY'LL PROBABLY GREASE THEM UP WITH SOME CASTOR OIL OR SOME BABY OIL, AND THAT COULD EASILY SHAVE ANOTHER 3/5 UP TO A FULL SECOND OFF....THIS ONE IS ON THE IMPROVE!!!! DEFINITE BET BACK !!!!!

#8 BADLANDS LEGACY- SEARS GAVE AN EXTREMELY WEAK DRIVE HERE ON A HORSE THAT WENT OFF AS THE 3-1 2ND CHOICE. HAD SOME GOOD LATE "POP", AND I'D LOVE TO SEE THIS ONE DRAW IN AWAY FROM #6.

5TH.....NTR

6TH......#7 SHAYNA BABY- GOT ROBBED OUT OF A WIN, BECAUSE ANDY MILLER LET THE RAIL OPEN UP IN THE FINAL 100 YARDS, AND
THERE WAS ABSOLUTELY NO REASON FOR HIM TO GO A 27.3 3RD QUARTER....THERE WAS NOBODY REALLY COMING AT HER, AWFUL DRIVE!!!!!! BET BACK, FOR SURE!!!!

7TH.....#11 SNAZZY HOT ROD - ANOTHER AWFUL DRIVE!!!!! TIMMY T. SHOULD HAVE HIS LICENSE RIPPED-UP AFTER THE TROUBLE HE PUT THIS GUY THROUGH.....THIS   GUY   WAS   TONS   THE BEST..........A MUST BET BACK, NEXT WEEK!!!!!!

8TH.......NTR

9TH......#9 CLOONEY DRUMMOND - 15-1 MORNING LINE HORSE, WAS BET DOWN TO AS LOW AS 9-5, FLOATED UP TO 7-2, AND WON. NOW, I MENTION THIS GUY FOR TWO REASONS......A. HE'S VERY "RAMMY-GATED" AND I THINK HE'D FAIR A LOT BETTER AT FREEHOLD (THAT'S WHERE I'D LIKE TO SEE HIM RACE NEXT).
FOR MANY YEARS NOW (AT LEAST SINCE THE YEAR 2000), THESE HORSES THAT ARE 20-1 OR 15-1 THAT TAKE A TON OF EARLY MONEY, AT THE BIG-M ALWAYS SEEM TO WIND-UP 1ST OR 2ND!!!!!!!

Signed,
Joseph J Tuttle

This kind of diligent videotape analysis (whether you decide to pay me to do the brain work for you or not) can only help secure more winning bets, for YOU, if you're willing to stay disciplined to this practice. I personally have been doing it (either through race replay shows or through the Internet), since 1997.

And, in a little over a decade, I can honestly say that my percentage of winning bets and my ability to find double-digit priced winners has gone up considerably. As it has been a direct result of implementing this practice into my handicapping, that has made me so much more successful as a Horseplayer.

Chapter Six
Betting from Home

"I cannot underscore enough just how amazing, and how much more fulfilling, betting from one's home can be."

I became fully proficient at navigating my way through and around the Internet by 1996 (or about two years into its inception). Soon, I found myself immersed in a whole new world. I was wagering from the privacy of my home, and having a blast.

My health started to improve (apparently I was allergic to cigarette smoke), and within about 3 to 5 weeks, I was no longer taking allergy meds.

Plus, when you're at an actual racetrack venue, let's face it, you find yourself handling a lot of money, which can also lead to potentially getting sick.

Well enough of being Dr. Joe. I just wanted to make it abundantly clear for any of you allergy sufferers or persons with weak immune systems, that this is another one of the residual benefits from betting from one's home.

{Past Posting}

Although in the earlier years of betting on horse racing through the Internet this was a lot more prevalent, the opportunity still on occasion, does exist. "Past Posting" by the simplest of definitions, is when you bet on a race after knowing the result. The first online racing sports book that I ever dealt with (IslandCasino.com), became notorious for allowing this to happen. They simply didn't have the proper people in position to keep track of the MTP (Minutes to Post), or late scratches for that matter, and this allowed me (and countless others I'm sure), to take full advantage of these situations.

I can vividly remember betting Hawthorne one afternoon where a 37-1 shot wound up paying $77.00 even to win, and I had $40.00 to win on him some 30 or 40 seconds after he'd already crossed the finish line. This is something that is not possible, wagering at an actual racetrack venue, through commingled pools.

Below, I'm going to add an actual anecdote from my first book as to another shining example of why you should be betting from home with a legitimate online/offshore race book.

"Wagering from the privacy of your own home I find to be both relaxing and cathartic. I personally bet through an online sports book/race book by the name of www.Bodoglife.com.

Now the reason for me playing with this company besides the fact that the owner (Calvin Ayre) is a billionaire, is that their maxims on how much you can win per race/bet are so high at all the major racetracks. I almost find myself feeling guilty in the fact that whenever I do hit an exotic wager, I'm typically getting paid anywhere between 7 to 50 percent more on my returns, then I would be getting as a part of a commingled pool at an actual race track venue.

Example: One day in the not so distance past I was in a harness horse gambling sort of mood and I was betting on a little racetrack in upstate New York called Monticello. I got lucky and hit a $79 horse in the middle part of a pick-3. I was alive with the three post time favorites in the third and final part of that pick-3. Horse #1 was a morning line 6-1 shot who got bet down to 5-2.

The pick-3 with him was paying $450 for a $2 bet. Horse #2 was the 9-5-morning line favorite who went off at 2-1 odds, and the pick-3 with him was paying $900 for a $2 bet.

Lastly, horse #3 was 5-2 morning line and went off as the post time favorite from an unfavorable post position (the seven hole) at 4-5 odds. The pick-3 with him was also paying $900. So, I feel it is safe to assume that the entire pick-3 pool was certainly no more than about $1200 (which to my best estimation would be about right given the takeout percentage Monticello has on pick-3 wagers).

Now, had I made the same wager through an outlet with commingled pools, I think the pick-3 paying $450 would have been paying one third less (which is 33 percent more for me), and the two that were paying $900 would have only been paying $450 (which is 50% more for me). That is the benefit that I feel you can get through playing with www.Bodoglife.com."

I'm not allergic to money, and after reading this book, if you opt to become a Bodoglife client (such as myself), here is my reference number: P6EA66; Joseph J. Tuttle.

Another wonderful advantage of betting from home are the plethora of horse racing information products readily available on the Internet through websites such as www.drf.com, www.brisnet.com, and www.equibase.com. And, if I may elaborate in regard to the three sites that I just mentioned, all three have uniquely different qualities in the way in which you can construct the racing form to look, from its traditional newspaper style version.

If you're a speed figure guy, you can reconstruct the form to accentuate numbers that are above a prescribed number that you designate.

If you're a class guy and you're looking for dropdown horses at all times, again, you'll have the ability to construct the form to your own personal preference.

If there are multiple categories that you would like to accentuate in the way that you construct your form to look, by all means you'll have that option.

The one program that I would highly recommend above all others in having the ability to reconstruct the form to your individual liking, and to your preferences, is the "Formulator 4.1" program by DRF, which I talked about briefly in the opening of the book.

Chapter Seven
Wagering Strategies

In this chapter we're going to delve into a few basic hedging principals, along with actual strategies, which can be implemented on a daily/nightly basis at your favorite tracks.

{Win, Place, and Show}

Win, along with Place, and Show are the absolute basics in the world of wagering on horses. The only strategy that I can tell you about from my experience, when it comes to Win, Place, or Show betting, is that there isn't much to tell. But, that doesn't mean that there are not many useful situations/strategies that can be implemented in any one of those three formats.

Now on more than one occasion I've been straddled with the moniker "Mr. Hedge". I'm not ashamed of such a thing, nor should you be. Let's say hypothetically that you're alive with one horse in the final part of a pick-4 and that it's paying four thousand dollars.

Now let's say, in the fourth and final part of that pick-4, it's only a six horse field. You would be a fool not to have substantial WIN WAGERS on the remaining five horses. And, just in case your horse finishes off the board, maybe even bet a five-horse Trifecta box (which on a $1.00 scale is a $60 bet). I think I've given two very easily understandable examples above. Plus, I plan to go more in-depth on the concept of "hedging-out, later on in this chapter.

As far as Place and Show bets are concerned, the only time I ever make a Place or Show bet is when I see a "Bridge Jumper" (a "bridge jumper" is an individual who is willing to bet $10,000 or more to Place or Show on one horse, to get the minimum .05 on the dollar for their investment), but, I must admit I'm not always privy to such information because I'm rarely at the track physically, anymore.

But, if you're at the track and you see a sizable Place or Show wager go in on one particular horse, it would greatly behoove you to put a token $2.00 on each of the other horses racing in that race. Because, in the event that said horse does not come in second or third you're going to get paid an incredibly handsome return two or three times over.

I can remember one day at Dover Downs (a quaint little harness track in Delaware), somebody wagered $40,000 to Show on a horse (that was going to win for fun at the top of the stretch), but he went on to make a break and finished fourth. I personally had $5.00 to Show on the other eight horses, and I collected handsomely on three of them (for there were three different Show payouts), obviously the horse that won, the horse that finished second and the horse that Showed. All three horses paid over $200 to Show, and the actual Show horse, paid over $300.

I turned my $40 investment (or stab if you will), into a little over $1,800! Situations such as the anecdote above are going to be few and far between, but when they arise you should at least try and take a "stab" on the remaining horses in said race, on at least a $2.00 scale.

{Exacta and Trifecta Wagering}

Again, I feel the need to revert back to my first book, to share with those of you who did not buy my first book ("The Ultimate Guide to Handicapping The Horses"), a wonderful anecdotal story, which in theory, can also be utilized as an actual wagering strategy.

"It was a beautiful sunny day at Hollywood Park, in Inglewood, California. I had just placed a pick-4 wager using the 1,2,4,7 (as my selections in the 1st race, as part of the early pick four wager), and I had also used the numbers (2), (5) and (7) in my "place pick-all" wager. It was only a (7) horse field, so that means that there are only (42) possible exacta combinations.

Now, given the current configuration of said two wagers, I asked myself a very honest question..."What exacta combinations are out there which would kill both of my bets?" There were only four possibilities that could come in, and completely ruin me! How's that for "coverage"? The exacta combinations that were out there waiting to become my possible demise were the following four: (3-1, 3-6, 6-1 or 6-3).

It was early in the day, and I had gotten crushed to the tune of $544.00 just the previous day. So, I had only invested $64.00 total in those two wagers, and because I wanted to get off on the proverbial "right foot", I decided to wager $10.00 a piece on those four possible killer combinations.

Long story short...the (3-6) exacta came in, and paid a whopping $90.20!!! I cashed for a little over $450.00 and found myself ahead $347.00 after just one race."

Because I enjoy wagering on the "Place Pick All" (even though I realize it's a bit of a sucker bet), I've used the above-mentioned "wagering strategy", on an every day basis, whenever I'm betting any tracks that have a "Place Pick All" (tracks such as Hawthorne, Hollywood Park, Santa Anita, and Golden Gate Fields). I've implemented the strategy that I stumbled across that day, everyday since, and so should you.

{Trifectas}…How one should incorporate "coverage" into hitting them!

I'm not a huge proponent of betting Trifectas, unless you're going to implement (and take full use of), "The All Button".

It's my personal belief that Exacta and Trifecta wagering are "sucker bets", as straight plays!

Now, what I mean by a "straight play" on an Exacta or Trifecta is the following: Playing a favorite on top in one straight Exacta or Trifecta, such as 6-4 or 6-4-1 (and other varying combinations in the "straight" format), is simply throwing good money after bad.

But, if you were to employ the use of "coverage" in making those types of wagers, I feel you'd start to hit them a lot more often. Assuming, that Exacta and Trifecta wagering is your personal preference. If it is, I think you might want to start wagering a little like this: $1.00 tri-key part-wheel, (6 with 1,2,3,4,5 with 1,2,3,4,5). This particular wager is only a $20.00 bet.

And, assuming that you are not using the favorite on top in this type of "tri-key part-wheel", chances are if (2) of your remaining (5) horses end up coming in 2nd and 3rd, you are going to cash a pretty nice ticket.

Especially, if the favorite is one of your "wheel" horses, but runs 3rd, or better still, out of the money! Another method that I like to utilize when wagering on a Trifecta, or an Exacta for that matter, is the word "all" or "all with all".

Example:

A $1.00 tri-wheel in an (9) horse race in which I were to call out something like...Give me a $1.00 tri, number (6), with "all"(for 2nd place), with "all" (for the show position). And, in case you are wondering, the wager above is a $56.00 bet.

Now, in the event that your "key" horse (the "key" horse is the one which you need to win), were to actually win, and it is the post time favorite, it can still pay handsomely. If by playing the "all" ticket you were to have a few long shots finish 2nd and 3rd, it could easily pay in the four or five hundred dollar range. Even if you "key" the favorite, and the 2nd choice ends up finishing in 2nd, as long as a 10-1 shot or higher is 3rd, you're probably going to make a small profit, on your $56.00 investment.

Naturally, "The All Ticket" can get very expensive in races that are larger than just a nine-horse field. On that note, it is my solemn belief that you should only "key" a horse that is 6-1 or higher, to truly insure a respectable return, if the field size is larger than nine horses.

If the field is eight horses or less I will not wager into that Trifecta pool, ever!

{How I hit the Pick-3's and Pick-4's}

Since I consider myself such an expert in the world of pick-3's and pick-4's I will now elaborate by showing a few different techniques.

I've tried to make it abundantly clear throughout the writing of this book exactly what kind of an utter love I have for pick-3's and pick-4's, and if you have not picked-up on that yet, you will now.

Because I feel as though my expertise lies not only in having a horsemanship background (because of my Father, Seymour Tuttle), but also due to the fact that over the last 10 years I feel as though I have truly mastered the art of properly configuring winning pick-3 and pick-4 tickets. The first step in properly configuring a winning pick-3 or pick-4 ticket is to know how much one needs, and/or should invest.

Whenever anyone talks about "guaranteed pools", (it typically means "better value" for us, the gamblers). Now, let's say I'm betting Hollywood Park and the "guaranteed early pick-4 pool" is $150,000. I can automatically assume that the pools are going to be larger than that number, and in all likelihood there will not be more than 1,000 total winning tickets.

This means, the minimum payback is going to be at least $150 (on a $1.00 ticket, in a world with no "takeout").

Now, that's an extremely conservative estimation that I constantly employ in my thinking, before I indulge in any exotic wager(s).

As a very basic rule of thumb you should never bet more into a race than ½ of 1/10 of one percent of the pool.

For example, (displayed in the table on the next page), are my stats from a small harness track up in Ohio, known as Northfield Park.

On a Friday night at Northfield Park, due to the influx of money coming in with out of state simulcast wagering, an average pick-3 pool at Northfield is somewhere in the neighborhood of $10,000 to $12,000 (with simulcast monies included), and if a pool is $12,000, then you would cut that number in half and that would equal 6,000, then, you would proceed to calculate 1/10th of one percent (of that half of the total pool number), which was 12,000, and that would equal exactly $6.00 in this instance.

This is a track that I don't even take seriously (and the stats shown are over the last year and a half of betting solely on pick-3's at Northfield Park racetrack). This is also a track with much smaller pools than most of your upper echelon thoroughbred facilities, and 12.23% is basically me only hitting one out of every eight wagers made.

Notice the profit/loss column displayed. The truly astonishing thing about the stats below is that my average wager size was well below $20 ($12.53 to be exact, per bet).

# of Bets	Win %	$1 ROI	Wagered	Payoff	Profit/Loss
319	12.23%	+0.30	$4013.00	$5213.70	$+1200.70

Now, as you can clearly see from the above-mentioned $12.53 average bet size on my pick-3's at Northfield Park, I tried to stay disciplined to the 1/2, of the pool size; 1/10th of one percent of the total pick-3 pool, wagering strategy. I never went over by more than $6 to $7 on average, which I feel is highly acceptable to do, when the pools are so small. Plus, I feel one should not be on the frugal side when it comes to trying to hit a pick-3 or pick-4.

{Superfectas}

Are they just a "sucker bet"?

My answer to that question above (about two years ago), use to be a very emphatic "yes"! But, with the advent of the "ten-cent Superfecta", there is now a reason to get involved with such a wager.

The "ten-cent Super" (as it is referred to at most tracks), allows one to invest a very small amount, while utilizing "coverage" to a degree not previously afforded to the masses.

When should one wager on a "Superfecta"?

I believe that the superfecta is a "fun wager", especially in the 0.10 formats. You shouldn't be looking for a "Huge Score" when betting the "Ten-Cent Super", primarily because you are only going to receive one-tenth of the $1.00 payout. So, if said Super were to pay $1,200.00, you are only going to get back a payout of $120.00. Now, the "upside" to this is you might only have to make a ten or twelve dollar wager to make that $120.00. Plus, in the "Ten-Cent" format you really can garner some amazing "coverage", and on the next page is just one prime example.

Example:

If you just want to pick out the horse that you think is likely to win said race, and use him or her as your "key" horse (to be played as the 1st place finisher only), at the top of your ticket, with the same (6) horses to be played in the 2nd, 3rd, and 4th positions, the ticket in question would cost precisely $12.00, and it would look something like this...(see below?)

An actual 0.10 "superfecta key wheel".

#1 (to actually win said race.)
with
2,3,4,5,6,7 (any (3) of these (6) numbers must finish 2nd, 3rd, or 4th,)
with
2,3,4,5,6,7 (any (3) of these (6) numbers must finish 2nd, 3rd, or 4th)
with
2,3,4,5,6,7 (any (3) of these (6) numbers must finish 2nd, 3rd, or 4th)

Now, as long as your "key" horse wins, and (3) of your (6) auxiliary selections for positions 2nd, 3rd, and 4th actually come in 2nd, 3rd, and 4th, then, you would win (1-6-4-7 would be a winning combination in the above-mentioned wager).

I'm not a very big proponent of wagering on any type of superfecta, but on occasion I will indulge just a bit, on a wager like the one shown above. But, I truly believe this method of superfecta wagering (as a strategy), is most likely your best chance at scoring for big money, without having to invest a lot.

In closing this chapter on "Wagering Strategies", I'd like to make one more thing abundantly clear... If you find yourself at all overwhelmed by some of my strategic maneuvers, feel free to drop me a line at my primary email address.

jjtuttle131@yahoo.com

Chapter Eight
Proper Money Management

Needless to say, this chapter will be short and to the point. Money Management is by far and away the most common shortcoming of at least 95 percent of the gamblers that I meet and/or know. Tell me if this sounds familiar; you're at the track, you're down a couple of hundred after a couple of hours and you see a horse going off at 5-2 that should be even money? So, you decide that you're going to try and get your two hundred dollars back, plus make a little profit by betting a hundred dollars on this 5-2 shot's nose. Instead of asking the most obvious question in the world, why is a horse that I think should be even money, going off at 5-2?

Could something be "wrong" with this horse? And because you didn't ask that question (or many others), you bet on him/her anyway. Needless to say this 5-2 shot that you thought was a gift from God, doesn't even hit the board. And, it's because you did not ask yourself the most obvious question(s), which I'm about to laid out.

I feel it's vitally important to constantly scrutinize decisions made on straight win bets in this wonderful world of horse racing. The more questions you ask and the more thorough you are, the better your overall results are going to be. So, now you find yourself down three hundred for the day because you just lost another hundred dollars in a matter of minutes. And, the primary reason why? You simply didn't ask enough questions.

Questions like: Was there a negative jockey change? Is the horse coming back too soon? Has his/her workout pattern changed? Is said horse dropping in class so much, that you should actually question the horse's soundness? These are all incredibly pertinent questions that need to be asked on a race-by-race basis, (with every horse), in each and every race that you handicap.

The above-mentioned example that I just wrote about is literally just one of many that I could talk about in greater detail if I chose to do so. But, now I'm going to get down to the brass tact facts of exactly what I think my definition of money management is. Now as I discussed slightly in the previous chapter, about the "two-percent rule", I do not subscribe to that at all.

It's a good rule if you're a family man who is NOT looking to subsidize one's income and/or to try to become a professional horseplayer.

But, if you want to give yourself a fair shot after reading this book, then, at the risk of sounding redundant, but you're going to need between a $5,000 to $7,000 bankroll. So now what Mr. Tuttle, you might ask yourself, after you've come up with the necessary funds? Well my retort is quite simple: If you read the book from cover to cover and you mange your money properly, you'll start winning a lot more than you lose. At the very least, if you don't find yourself making consistent daily profits, you will undoubtedly be helping your cause by stretching out the length of time your bankroll normally would last you.

Here's how I "manage" my money. If I'm going to be spending a day at the racetrack, I first determine what two tracks (at the most two) I'm going to be wagering on throughout the day. Then, I decide to allocate to the exact dollar, how much money I'm going to need to make the necessary wagers I want to make between the two cards for that day. Personally, I love pick-3's and pick-4's.

Now hypothetically, if the two tracks in question have rolling pick-3's and say for instance two pick-4's on each individual racing program, I will bet all four pick-4's and probably a grand total of four pick-3's between the two tracks. In the event my eight total wagers amass $798, then so be it.

In the world of "guaranteed pools" at some of your bigger racetracks such as Santa Anita, Hollywood Park, Belmont, etc., with these types of exotic wagers, you only need to win about 14 percent of them (or 1 out of every 7) to consistently stay afloat and/or make a little profit. Now, when I talk about "guaranteed pools", let's say I'm betting Hollywood Park and the guaranteed early pick-4 pool is $150,000.   I can automatically assume that the pools are going to be larger than that number, and in all likelihood there will not be more than 1,000 total winning tickets. This means, the minimum payback is going to be at least $150; on a $1.00 ticket.

Now that's an extremely conservative estimation that I constantly employ in my thinking. As a very basic rule of thumb you should never bet more into a race than ½ of 1/10 of one percent of the pool.

So, if I'm "at the track", and I can visually see the money being bet and I can visually see the pools, and I see the early pick-4 pool being $222,000, I can safely and in good conscience wager $111 or less, knowing that even if I lose, I'm saving money quite possibly for a future wager. The way that I derived $111 as the maximum size of my wager, is precisely ½ of the pool size, (111,000), and then calculating 1/10, of one percent, thereafter.

{For those of you who don't know how to calculate how much a particular pick-3 or pick-4 is going to cost you, it is really quite simple. It's just simple multiplication. Let's say we're constructing a pick-4. On a $1 scale, 4 horses x 4 horses x 4 horses x 1 horse (in the final part) would simply be a cost of $64 (4 x 4 x 4 x 1).}

Most "professionals" rely too much on feel and not enough on mathematics, when constructing a pick-3 or pick-4 wager. A shining example of what I'm talking about would be the following: if I can construct a pick-4 wager of two horses, with four horses, with four horses again in the third leg, with a single in the final leg, which is only a cost of $32. At that point, I then need to make the determination in which leg or legs I should give myself more "coverage". At which point I intentionally increase the size of my wager, yet still try and stay under $111.

Example:

Five horses, with five horses, with three horses, with one, would now end up being a $75 bet. I've now more than doubled my original wager size and given myself the piece of mind of added "coverage".

It's been my experience, that as I'm adding horses and "coverage" to my wager, I find myself intentionally seeking out "rank outsiders" (horses that are 10-1 morning line or higher). This gives me a much better chance at one of these "rank outsiders" winning for me, which in turn, can increase my payback potential, in the event that I go on to win that particular wager.

In closing, I do believe the old adage, "bet with your head, not over it", still applies to all of us regardless of experience level, innate natural ability levels, and/or no matter how financially secure you believe yourself to be. Which leads me to my final point, "chasing". "Chasing" is an affliction that can rare it's ugly head on best of us.

My definition of "chasing" is probably the same definition everybody else has of it. It's simply trying too hard to win your way out of a losing streak. If you ever find yourself or feel like you might be in "chase mode", it may be time to walk away for a few weeks. Not days, but weeks! Now I know that might sound a little redundant, but it's the best advice I can offer.

I've seen "chasing" first hand turn a guy that was worth a million dollars into a homeless person inside of a year. And, it's because he didn't obey the golden rule. "Always, bet with your head, not over it."

Chapter Nine
Equipment and Medications

One of the greatest advantages that I feel like I possess over 85% of the betting public is the ability to assess the way in which a horse is "hung-up".

"Hung-Up" is a bit of horsemanship vernacular, which is used in describing what equipment a horse is wearing during the score down or in the post parade (on a regular basis), prior to their race.

To have the ability to quickly disseminate this information in just a matter of moments is a colossal advantage. I hope that as you read this chapter, that you too will soon be able to put my horsemanship skills to proper use.

It's my solemn belief that through "understanding", anything can be taught or learned. And, I'm going to try my best to help you understand some of the most important aspects to horse racing (as it pertains to know what certain types of equipment and medications are primarily used for), that you've probably have not been privied to, in your lifetime.

The little lower case "b" next to the assigned weigh a horse carried last time out, stands for "Blinkers". As in the blinkers were "on" for that horse's last race. But, what the racing form always neglects to tell you; is exactly what "type" of Blinkers said horse was wearing! Think about it?

On the next page is a picture of one of the more common blinker types (known as the French/Quarter blinker), and it's just one of many that a horse could be wearing prior to any given race. Over the next few pages I will give a brief overview describing their usage(s). Each of these blinkers has a uniquely different intended purpose, and it's at the discretion of the trainer to know exactly which type his or her horse might need.

French/Quarter - (otherwise or better known as "cheater blinkers"). "Cheater blinkers" do have the ability to help sharpen one's speed, but its main intended use is to keep a horse more focused on the task at hand, and to still have the ability to see other horses coming.

The Half/Full – This blinker is the standard bearer, to simply "sharpen a horse's speed", and it clearly helps a horse pay more attention to the task at hand. This is the most commonly recognizable blinker used today. And, the one that you'll be exposed to the most. It extends out just a few centimeters more than the "Quarter".

Semi/Full ¾ - Again, this will help sharpen a horse's speed (in my humble opinion more so than the first two), and is probably the most common type of blinker that you will see on a bigger/less coordinated type of horse.

Extended or Scoop – this is a nearly full blinker/cup, which fits completely around and over 80% of the eye. You'll almost never see a horse wearing the "Extended or Scoop Blinker" on the sides of both eyes. I personally love to see this piece of equipment on the outside eye (outside eye being the horse's right eye if you were looking directly at said horse), and the reason that I love to see a horse "hung-up" like this, is because it's a bit of a tip off to me (as a horseman), that the trainer thinks his horse can clear off to the lead.

Then, when another horse challenges said horse, that complete inability to see any part of the horse (but only hear the other horse and/or jockey), will typically help scare said horse on to victory. When this piece of equipment happens to be on the "inside eye", it is done so to help alleviate said horse's possible fear of the rail, or in most cases, it is done because the horse likes to "bear out" in the turns or the stretch. I'm not as excited to see this piece of equipment utilized on the "inside eye", nearly as much as the outside.

Plexiglass (Amber, Green or Clear) – this is a full blinker/cup, which fits completely around and over the eye. Its primary function is to act as a windshield wiper (if you will), or to effectively help "braven-up" a horse that shies away from dirt in said horse's eyes. Those descriptions hold more so true for the Amber or Clear colored ones. The "Green" ones have been used a lot over time, as a way to "change a horse's perspective".

It might actually help calm said horse down, usually; a horse that wears the green ones will also wear "ears" ("ears" are a piece of equipment that I'll get into later on, made popular by the California horse trainer, Barry Abrams).

The Full Blind – typically, you'll see this in the color blue, and again, you'll only see it on one of the two eyes, instead of both. It is typically used for horses that suffer from "moon blindness". You'll notice this piece of equipment more so at racetrack venues that race at night rather than in the middle of the day. It's not a piece of equipment that you should be on the lookout for.

I'm a big believer that the shadow roll can greatly improve the performance of a horse (of a particular horse using it for the first time) especially if said horse is also adding, "1st time blinkers".

The obvious usage of the "Shadow Roll" is to help prevent a horse from "jumping shadows" (during the course of training or in a race). But, the real/underscored and typically not talked about, reason for its use with/for thoroughbred racehorses is to make a horse "stretch-out" (as in it lengthens their stride). And, if horse has this issue rectified (through the use of a shadow roll), it can lead to victory for said horse at first use.

{Bandages}

As a very simple rule of thumb (as both a gambler and a horseman), I do not like to see a horse that wears "four wraps" ("wraps" are bandages). You can make a very safe assumption, that a horse wearing four wraps either currently has some legitimate leg problems and/or has had leg issues in the past.

"Two wraps", especially if they are front wraps only, can also be very "eyebrow raising", and/or disturbing to see. "Front wraps only" (in two-year olds), is typically not a bad sign, it merely suggests to me, that it is being done as a precautionary measure.

"Hind wraps only" (in 90% of the cases of two and three year olds), is done primarily for one of two main reasons.

To ever so slightly change one's gate so that said horse does not interfere with itself, when in full stride, or it is being done to garner an added level of support (usually with much bigger horses, sixteen hands or more), for said horse's hindquarters, due to the fact that's where all thoroughbreds derive their power and/or stride capabilities, and stride characteristics. In older horses (four years old and up), seeing hind wraps only is actually a good thing.

Again, it reveals to me that the trainer of said horse feels the need to have them on his or her horse, for one of the above-mentioned reasons already given. In older horses especially, I would much rather see hind wraps only, than front wraps only. Especially, when I'm almost never at the track physically, and I only have my TVG satellite feed to help guide me as I'm watching post parades.

{"Rundown Wraps"}

"Rundown wraps" are generally on the hind legs only and they primarily only cover the ankle. Big Brown, wears rundown wraps on his hind legs, along with full bandages up front. So, to see a horse with that combination is obviously not necessarily a bad thing. Now, if you're still asking yourself what are rundown wraps, I'm here to tell you. When a horse is in full stride, and if they have long sloping pastern bones (the pastern connects the ankle to the hoof), generally speaking a horse's hind ankles will literally penetrate through the dirt, and to the surface core, which can lead to soreness and/or lameness in some horses.

Again, just like with the "shadow roll" this is a piece of equipment that can directly affect and/or improve a horse's performance immediately, and the information is not given to the general public.

Additionally, once a horse wears rundown wraps for the first time, typically said horse will always wear them prior to a race for the duration of its racing career. In the event that you were to notice them come off (more so on an older horse, than a younger one), and the horse is in good form, you can make the honest assertion that three to four fifths of a second could potentially be shaved off of said horse's time from its last race. So naturally being very astute (in your note taking practices), can reward you handsomely the first time you notice this piece of equipment as an addition to any horse, in your wagering endeavors.

One more thing... you're probably only going to be able make a potential "score" on a two-year old that you notice is wearing first time "rundowns". Now, in the event you see first time "rundowns" on an older horse (that was just recently claimed by a new trainer), this may very well be another situation to try and "pounce on".

{Shoeing}

As far as shoeing goes, I feel the need to make one small preface, by saying that "I'm no Ferrier"! But, what I do know about shoeing and what I can share will only help those of you that like to hang out down by the paddock, and watch the horses get saddled prior to a race.

This is due to the fact that every paddock in the country .has what's known as a "shoe board" (where you can actually see prior to a race what types of shoes each horse is wearing), and now you will actually be able to spend that time down there, a little more wisely.

Initially, when a young horse is in heavy training (trying to make it to the races for its first start), a trainer will opt for a stronger/sturdier type of shoe. Typically, the shoe used is a "full swedge" steel shoe.

Another reason for the full swedge steel shoe (at least during training prior to one's first start) is that they will be taken off for good about a day or two prior to said horse's first start. And in theory, the "lighter aluminum shoe" should shave a few fifths, all the way up to a full second, off of said horse's final time in that first start.

Having the knowledge of that little tidbit of information primarily will only help you when looking at workouts of first time starters, and only if the "spacing between workouts" is very stringent and uniformed.

When I use a phrase like "very stringent and uniformed", I'm referring to the workouts being placed about six to eight days apart from one another. *That is called quality spacing of workouts, and it is most certainly something you should look for in either young baby races, or upper echelon stakes races, when looking at the form on these two types of runners. Or, if a horse has had a prolonged amount of time away from the races, "quality spacing" is also something to look for.*

Sometimes (with smaller or somewhat frail horses), a trainer will opt to go directly to the lightweight aluminum shoes, for there is a lot less chance for future lameness's to occur during training. Whereas doing it the old fashioned way (above-mentioned), does have that one possible pitfall.

So, if you're someone who likes to bet on baby races and/or upper echelon stakes races, it would greatly behoove you to be cognizant of a horse's actual physical stature. These days, most of the pertinent information about shoeing is given to the general public (during pre-race shows), and for the most part the information can be beneficial, if you know the significance behind what said trainer might be trying to accomplish with said horse.

Example:

Say it's a muddy day at Belmont Park, and there have been a lot of scratches. Now let's say you're involved in a six-horse sprint race where all the horses are wearing either "stickers", "bends", or "mud calks".

In some cases, a horse might be wearing a combination of the three between front and back hooves. So what does it all mean from a handicapping perspective?

Not a whole hell of a lot if the track has been "sealed". If a track has been "sealed", any or all combinations are strictly being used for purposes of added traction.

The combination that I personally love to see the most (on a very "off", "soupy", or "sealed" racetrack), are "stickers up front" and "quarter inch bends" behind. This was a combination that my Father had a lot of success with, so I saw it work first hand.

At the time of the writing of this book (Sunday, May, 11, 2008), it is exactly six days before the Preakness Stakes, and the horse Big Brown is definitely going to be the overwhelming favorite. Big Brown has had a problem with his feet, with something known as "quarter cracks". A horse that has a "quarter crack" (in Big Brown's case he has it on more than one hoof), typically will wear what is known as a "bar shoe".

The "bar shoe" is just another, in a long line of pieces of equipment that help alleviate pain and/or facilitate added support.

Amongst stakes caliber horses, knowing that a horse is wearing one or more "bar shoes" does not bother me in the least, nor should it you. Now, if you're talking about a $5,000 claimer at Mountaineer, that's an entirely different scenario, and I would "stay away"!

In closing on the topic of shoeing, I don't feel it's very pertinent for someone who has no interest in becoming a future horseman (if your sole interest is strictly as a gambler), for purposes of handicapping. But if you consider yourself a very astute person, these little nuances will only help with future handicapping decisions, in either baby races or stakes races.

{"Atypical" pieces of equipment}

I briefly spoke earlier of a piece of equipment called "ears". "Ears" were introduced to us in the late 70's, early 80's by the California-based, Hall of Fame trainer, Barry Abrams. "Ears" were developed as a way to calm down an "incredibly rambunctious" or "easily scared" horse, without the use of any kind of sedatives. Quite simply, they are earmuffs for horses. The most famous horse that wore "ears" (if memory serves me correctly or at least in my lifetime) was Gate Dancer.

Ironically, enough he was trained by another very successful California-based trainer (or at least at the time), Jack Van Berg of Alysheba fame.

{The "tongue tie"}

I would venture a guess that somewhere in the neighborhood of 90 to 95% of all racehorses wear a "tongue tie".

The main usage for a "tongue tie" is to ensure that a horse does not get his tongue over the bit, for when that happens; nothing good can come of it.
A horse can quite literally swallow his own tongue and "choke down" (albeit this is very rare amongst thoroughbreds, and much more prevalent with standardbreds), or if the horse is able to get his tongue over the bit, he or she will become extremely hard to steer, and will almost certainly restrict said horse's airways and lead to an incredibly poor performance.

There has been a ton of rumor and innuendo for many years surrounding the "ability to lace" a tongue-tie, but I'm not a very big believer of it, nor should you be. One characteristic that I love to see (when either watching a horserace live or on video replay), is something known as a "tongue lollar".

A horse that is a "tongue lollar" races with most of his tongue out of his mouth (usually hanging towards the rail and/or said horse's left side), in such a relaxed manner that it exudes a certain level of class, in my humble opinion. It's simply a characteristic that I've noticed over the years (amongst horses that wear tongue ties), of horses that are very game and/or determined at all times.

Just another little something that you should look for, the next time that you are watching a two horse battle down the stretch!

{Figure Eight noseband}

A "figure eight" noseband is a leather strap that goes over the bridge of a horse's nose to help secure the bridle.

A "figure eight" noseband goes over the bridge of the nose and under the rings of the bit to help keep the horse's mouth closed. This keeps the tongue from sliding up over the bit, and is used on horses that do not like having a tongue-tie used. This is not to say that a horse cannot wear/use both in conjunction with one another.

As a basic rule of thumb if I see a horse wearing both a "figure eight" and a tongue-tie, I can safely make the assumption that the horse may have some issues with sometimes being rank. Or, he may have a tendency to want to run with his mouth wide open, which can make it very hard for the rider to steer the horse. And, it can also make it quite hard for the horse to breathe properly.

But, if after watching said horse run, and I do not notice any "rankness", I will make a note of it and look for one of the two to come off in said horse's next subsequent start.

{Shadow Rolls}

On thoroughbreds there are primarily just two types of "Shadow Rolls" that are used.

There are thin ones and thick ones. *(A roll is usually made of sheepskin that is secured over the bridge of a horse's nose to keep it from seeing shadows on the track and shying away from or jumping them).*

You won't find it (Shadow Rolls) listed in a program or past performance lines like Lasix, blinkers, and front wraps. I have no idea why it isn't! It can help a horse immensely, if they truly need it. And, I feel that this one piece of equipment must become an integral part of your note-taking processes.

You need to make a very concerted effort in adding this practice to your everyday note-taking, because, it might be a good idea to take note (in your program or notebook), of each horse wearing a shadow roll, because, when you finally come across a horse wearing one (that wasn't wearing it in its previous start), there very well could be the potential for a score!

{The "breast collar"}

This is a seldom-used piece of equipment (in the year 2008), but as a basic rule of thumb, it is simply used to ensure that the saddle doesn't slip, on said horse.

I'm of the opinion that if a horse needs a "breast collar" in the year 2008, he or she probably does not want to be a racehorse. A very basic, yet accurate inference (from a horsemanship standpoint), that one can make about a horse that wears a "breast collar", is that either A. said horse really doesn't want the saddle on them (which suggests to me that the horse is a little "classless" and doesn't truly want to be a racehorse), or B. the horse simply has a very small girth (which a lot of old time horseman will tell you is a "tale tell sign" that the horse is lacking in "ability"), and I certainly do subscribe to the parenthetic statement prior of what a lot of older horseman think.

{Medications}...Usages and Pertinence in Handicapping

Essentially, there are only two specific medications that you need to know about and/or that are published in the form, that racehorses are given. The older of the two medications is Phenylbutazone (more commonly known as "Bute").

Basically Bute is used primarily as an anti-inflammatory and/or fever-reducer much like aspirin for a human being.

The other commonly known medication that is printed in the Racing Form on a daily basis is Furosemide (otherwise known as "Lasix"), and as of the writing of this book, about 80% of all racehorses use this medication, both in training and in racing.

{Lasix}

I wrote in my first book that I believed Lasix should become mandatory and I will now show you an excerpt from my first book that better conveys how I feel towards the topic of Lasix, and in regards to it's usage in racehorses.

Excerpt from "The Ultimate Guide to Handicapping the Horses"... *"I believe that number needs to be at 100%! The reason why I think Lasix is not "overused", and should become mandatory, is due to the fact that almost all horse's "bleed" a little bit (especially during the stresses of going all-out during the running of a race), and it just seems to be a bit more humane, in my opinion.* **But, there are still owners of racehorses out there that believe the use of this medication diminishes the overall value of the horse, in the event that said horse were to go on and have a career as a stud.**

It's my opinion that an owner that still subscribes to such a view, might want to consider a new hobby, or at least become more educated about the topic.

It's my contention that "1st time Lasix" no longer has the same effect it once had in the world of handicapping. It's my solemn belief from a handicapping perspective that "2nd time Lasix" is a much more valuable "Angle" to consider.

In my opinion, 2nd time Lasix is a much stronger position to help base a selection on. There are a few crucial variables that most horseplayer's are not aware of. Such as, the fact that in most states horses racing on the medication Lasix must receive it in a "Detention Barn".

And, there's the fact that when getting this medication for the first time, said horse might not urinate most of it out of his/her system in time for their race.

Lasix is a diuretic and a horse on it should urinate a lot, prior to going to the paddock for saddling. Naturally, the first time this completely foreign substance is injected into a horse, the horse may not totally "go" enough prior to the start of the race.

As of consequence, the horse may not race as well, as compared to the second time around. If said horse showed a marked improvement after the first start with the Lasix, then you can rest assured, that the second time will probably garner even more favorable results."

{Bute}

Probably the most common used medication in horses, primarily used as an anti-inflammatory drug for swelling, musculoskeletal pain and fever. Bute is very effective for injury and lameness, and no other non-steroidal agent has been shown more effective that is not any more inexpensive, than Bute.

Typically when looking at horses PP's, if you see an "L" and then next to it a "B", that means that the horse is also on a steady diet of "Bute" prior to each race. To my knowledge (at the time of the writing of this book), both of these medications are 100% legal in every state where there is racing in the U.S. and Canada.

But, not all racing states allow "Bute" to be used just prior to the horse getting ready for an upcoming race. Some states want a horse's "Bute" level to be below a certain point, and recommend that it not be given to said horse either 48 or 72 hours prior to their upcoming race.

In closing this chapter, I'd like to reiterate that these are primarily the only two medications that you're going to be exposed to on a regular basis, when reading the Racing Form.

Additionally, I would strongly advise reading my thoughts and opinions (the italicized excerpt above from my first book), to more accurately understand my thought processes, as a handicapper, as it pertains to these medications.

Chapter Ten

What does it all mean?
(Philosophies put into practical use)

Well, if you've gotten this far and you've enjoyed and/or feel as though you've learned a few things, your education through "The Tuttle Way" is about to take a colossal leap forward.

Now I make a very consorted effort (in the way that I write), to make it seem as though as you are reading, it almost feels as though I am talking to you. Now there is a real method to my madness here, and it was my ultimate goal to write in this manner, for I truly believe that my teachings will only illuminate whatever handicapping prowess you already posses, even further.

I'm a huge proponent of something that I've classified as "Line Interpretation". I talked about "Line Interpretation" ad nauseam on my first ever online website (that was up and running from 1998 to 2001), www.themaddcapper.com.

Now granted, that was a sports handicapping website. But, I still feel as though its basic premise can be applied to making better decisions when handicapping horse races.

Example:

I guess the "double bet down theory" would be the least elaborate example that I can give you. The "double bet down theory" (which is one of the thirteen "Angles" that I talked about in great detail, in my first book), is an extremely rudimentary way to expound upon "Line Interpretation".

The "double bet down theory" works something like this... You're at home one day betting on some races (the track that you are betting is of no consequence), and you notice a horse at 7-2, that was 22-1 in his or her last start. Additionally, said horse had a morning line of 8-1, what are we to make of this? In my world, if there is still two or three minutes before post time and I notice this, I would strongly suggest that you do what I would do, and perform some further investigating. Because clearly this is a horse that falls under the criteria (that by my definition), is a "double bet down horse".

This is an "Angle" that you need to stay very cognizant of at all times, especially at cheaper racetrack venues. Places such as Calder Race Course, Finger Lakes, Mountaineer, etc.

Even though it pains me to do this, I'm going to let you see another excerpt from my first book to better illustrate how one can put full usage of the "double bet down theory" to work, for you.

Excerpt from "The Ultimate Guide to Handicapping the Horses":

".... Let's say the horse is not dropping significantly in class, there has been no significant trainer or jockey change, and/or equipment change, yet the horse is for some unknown reason going off at 9-2. This is what is known as a "hot horse", or a horse that meets the criteria for the "double bet down" theory.

Now with horses like these, it's sometimes hard to make a case for them, yet there it is right before your eyes, the horse has been bet down from his/her last start, it's been bet down from the morning line, even though his/her past performance lines (at least recently), may not look very appealing, the horse in question is still getting bet.

At this point, the question "why" can probably be answered through watching this particular horse's last couple of outings, through "race replay". If after watching said horse's last two starts, and you still can't see a legitimate reason "why" the horse is getting bet, then I would strongly suggest that you just stay away from that horse. But, if you're investigating (from watching the race replays) does reveal something significant, I'd advise you to lay a fairly sizable win wager on this kind of a horse, and simply "trust" the steady flow of money coming in on said horse."

The italicized portion above may come off as a little "anal-retentive", but this is the kind of discipline necessary, in order to become a winning horseplayer. It is my solemn belief (and probably always will be), that ANYONE can "turn it all around" at any given moment, and in my world there is no time like the present.

So, if you're reading this and you've been a "perennial loser" for most of your life as a horseplayer (or even as a gambler in general), I steadfastly hold resolute in my belief of what I just said.

And on that note, here is my primary e-mail address (jjtuttle131@yahoo.com). Feel free to write me with any questions at any time.

Signed,
Joseph J. Tuttle

Complete Alphabetical Index of Horse Terminology

ALLOWANCE

A race other than a claiming event for which the racing secretary drafts certain conditions to determine weights to be carried based on the horse's age, sex and/or past performance.

ALSO-ELIGIBLE

A horse officially entered for a race, but not permitted to start unless the field is reduced by scratches below a specified number.

APPRENTICE

A jockey who has ridden for less than a year and who receives weight allowances.

APPRENTICE ALLOWANCE

Weight concession given to an apprentice rider of ten pounds until the fifth winner, seven pounds until the 35th winner, five pounds after the 35th winner. The apprentice is then allowed five pounds for one calendar year after the 40th winner beginning with the date of the 5th winner.

BACKSTRETCH

Straight portion of the far side of the racing surface between the turns.

BANDAGE (otherwise known as a "wrap")

Leg wraps used for support or protection against injury during a race.

BAR SHOE

A horseshoe closed at the back to help support the heel of the hoof. Often worn by horses with quarter cracks or bruised feet.

BAY

A color ranging from tan to dark chestnut with black mane, tail and points.

BEYER SPEED RATING

A measure of performance popularized by Andy Beyer of The Washington Post

BIT

A stainless steel, rubber or aluminum bar, attached to the bridle, which fits in the horse's mouth and is one the means by which a jockey exerts guidance and control.

BLACK

A horse color which is black, including the muzzle, flanks, mane, tail and legs unless white markings are present.

BLEEDER

A horse that bleeds from the lungs when small capillaries that surround the lungs' air sacs (alveoli) rupture. The medical term is "exercise-induced pulmonary hemorrhage" (EIPH). The most common treatment is the use of the diuretic furosemide (Lasix).

BLINKERS

A cup-shaped device to limit a horse's vision to prevent him from swerving from objects or other horses on either side of him.

BLOW-OUT

A short, timed workout, usually a day or two before a race, designed to sharpen a horse's speed. Usually three-eights on either side of it.

BOLT

Sudden veering from a straight course, usually to the outside rail.

BOUNCE

An exceptionally poor performance on the heels of an exceptionally good one

BOWED TENDON

A type of tendonitis. The most common injury to the tendon is a strain or "bowed" tendon, so named because of the appearance of a bow shape due to swelling.

BREAK MAIDEN

Horse or rider winning the first race of its career.

BREEZE or BREEZING

Working a horse at moderate speed.

BRIDLE

A piece of equipment usually made of leather or nylon, which fits on a horse's head and is where other equipment, such as a bit and the reins, are attached.

BROODMARE

A female horse used for breeding.

BROODMARE SIRE

A sire whose female offspring become producers of exceptional performers.

BUG BOY

An apprentice rider.

BULLET

Fastest workout of the day at a particular distance.

BULLRING

A small racetrack, usually less than one mile.

BUTE

Short for phenylbutazone, a non-steroidal anti-inflammatory medication that is legal in most racing jurisdictions. Often known by the trade names Butazolidin and bute.

CALK

A projection on the heels of a horseshoe, similar to a cleat, on the rear shoes of a horse to prevent slipping, especially on a wet track. Also known as a "sticker." Sometimes incorrectly spelled "caulk."

CALL TO THE POST

A special call played on a Bugle used to signal the horses to the starting gate.

CANNON BONE

The third metacarpal (front leg) or metatarsal (rear leg), also referred to as the shin bone. The largest bone between the knee and ankle joints.

CHALK

Wagering favorite in a race. Dates from the days when on-track bookmakers would write current odds on a chalkboard.

CHECK(ED)

When a jockey slows a horse due to other horses impeding its progress.

CHESTNUT

A color ranging from light gold to deep red. Also, a small, horny growth on the inside of a horse's front legs.

CLAIM OR CLAIMING

Process by which a licensed person may purchase a horse entered in a designated race for a predetermined price. When a horse has been claimed, its new owner assumes title after the starting gate opens although the former owner is entitled to all purse money earned in that race.

CLAIMING RACE

A race in which the horses are for sale at a price specified before the race. Claims are made before the race and the new owner assumes possession immediately following the race.

A "CLASSIC" Race

1: A race of traditional importance 2: Used to describe a distance, i.e., a race at the American classic distance, which is 1 1/4 miles.

CLIMBING

When a horse lifts its front legs abnormally high as it gallops, causing it to run inefficiently.

CLUBHOUSE TURN

The turn on a racing oval that is closest to the clubhouse facility usually the first turn after the finish line.

COLT

A male horse 3 years old or younger.

CONDITION BOOK(S)

A series of booklets issued by a racing secretary, which set forth conditions of races to be run at a particular racetrack.

CONDITIONS

The requirements of a particular race. This may include age, sex, money or races won, weight carried and the distance of the race.

CONDYLAR FRACTURE

A fracture in the lower knobby end (condyle) of the lower (distal) end of a long bone such as the cannon bone or humerus (upper front limb).

COUPLED (ENTRY)

Two or more horses running as an entry in a single betting unit.

CUPPY (TRACK)

A dry and loose racing surface that breaks away under a horse's hooves.

DAM

The mother of a horse.

DARK BAY OR BROWN

A horse color that ranges from brown with areas of tan on the shoulders, head and flanks, to a dark brown, with tan areas seen only on the flanks and/or muzzle. The mane, tail and lower portions of the legs are always black unless white markings are present.

DECLARED

In the United States, a horse withdrawn from a stakes race in advance of scratch time. In Europe, a horse confirmed to start a race.

DISTAFF

A race for female horses.

DOGS (otherwise known as "working around the dogs")

Rubber traffic cones (or a wooden barrier) placed at certain distances out from the inner rail, when the track is wet, muddy, soft, yielding or heavy, to prevent horses during the workout period from churning the footing along the rail.

DRIVING

Strong urging by jockey to.

DWELT

Extremely late in breaking from the gate.

EARLY FOOT

Good speed at the start of a race.

ENTRY

Two or more horses representing the same owner or trained by the same person and running together as a single betting entity.

FAST TRACK

Footing that is dry, even and resilient.

FETLOCK

Joint located between the cannon bone and the long pastern bone, also referred to as the "ankle."

FIELD HORSE or MUTUEL FIELD

Two or more starters running as a single betting unit (entry), when there are more starters in a race than positions on the tote board.

FILLY

A female horse less than 5 years old.

FIRM TRACK

A condition of a turf course corresponding to fast on a dirt track. A firm, resilient surface.

FLATTEN OUT

A very tired horse that slows considerably.

FURLONG

An eighth of a mile.

FUROSEMIDE

A medication used in the treatment of bleeders, commonly known under the trade name Lasix, which acts as a diuretic, reducing pressure on the capillaries.

FUTURITY

A race for two-year-olds in which the owners make a continuous series of payments over a period of time to keep their horses eligible. Purses for these races vary but can be considerable.

GELDING

A neutered male horse.

GIRTH

An elastic and leather band sometimes covered with sheepskin that passes under a horse's belly and is connected to both sides of the saddle.

GOOD TRACK

A dirt track that is almost fast or a turf course slightly softer than firm.

GRAB A QUARTER (which can lead to "quarter cracks")

Injury to the back of the hoof or foot caused by a horse stepping on itself (usually affects the front foot). Being stepped on from behind in the same manner, usually affects the back foot. A common, usually minor injury.

GRADED RACE

Established in 1973 to classify select stakes races in North America, at the request of European racing authorities, who had set up group races two years earlier. Capitalized when used in race title (the Grade I Belmont Stakes). See group race.

GRAY

A horse color where the majority of the coat is a mixture of black and white hairs. The mane, tail and legs may be either black or gray unless white markings are present. Starting with foals of 1993, the color classifications gray and roan were combined as "roan or gray." See roan.

HALTER

Like a bridle, but lacking a bit. Used in handling horses around the stable and when they are not being ridden.

HAND

Four inches. A horse's height is measured in hands and inches from the top of the shoulder (withers) to the ground, e.g., 15.2 hands is 15 hands, 2 inches. Thoroughbreds typically range from 15 to 17 hands.

HANDICAPPING

This is the study of factors in the past performances, which determine the relative qualities and abilities of horses in a race.

HANDLE

Money wagered.

HEAVY TRACK

Wettest possible condition of a turf course; not usually found in North America.

HOCK

A large joint just above the shin bone in the rear legs. Corresponds to the level of the knee of the front leg.

HORSE

When reference is made to sex, a "horse" is an ungelded male five-years-old or older.

HOT WALKER

The person who walks the horses to cool them down after a workout or a race.

IN THE MONEY

Finishes first, second or third.

INFIELD

Area encompassed by the inner rail of the turf course.

INQUIRY

Official investigation of rules infractions.

IRONS

See "Stirrups"

ITW

Intertrack wagering.

JUVENILE

Two-year-old horse.

LASIX

Diuretic medication given to horses which bleed.

LENGTH

A measurement approximating the length of a horse, used to denote distance between horses in a race.

LISTED RACE

A stakes race just below a group race or graded race in quality.
MAIDEN

A horse that hasn't won a flat race in any country.
MARE

A female horse 5 years old or older.
MIDDLE DISTANCE

Broadly, from one mile to 1 1/8 miles.
MORNING LINE

The starting odds set by the track handicapper.
MUDDY TRACK

A condition of a racetrack, which is wet but has no standing water.
NOSE BAND (the most common nose band used on thoroughbreds today, is known as the "figure eight" nose band)

A leather strap that goes over the bridge of a horse's nose to help secure the bridle. A "figure eight" nose band goes over the bridge of the nose and under the rings of the bit to help keep the horse's mouth closed. This keeps the tongue from sliding up over the bit and is used on horses that do not like having a tongue tie used.

OBJECTION

Claim of a foul lodged by a rider, patrol judge or other official after the running of a race. If lodged by an official, it is called an inquiry.
ODDS-ON

Odds of less than even money (as in 4-5, 3-5, or less at post time).
OFF-TRACK BETTING

Wagering at legalized betting outlets usually run by the tracks, management companies specializing in pari-mutuel wagering or, in New York State, by independent corporations chartered by the state. Wagers at OTB sites are usually commingled with on-track betting pools.

OVERLAY

A horse whose odds are greater than its potential to win.

OVERNIGHT RACE

A race in which entries close a specific number of hours before running (such as 48 hours), as opposed to a stakes race, for which nominations close weeks and sometimes months in advance.

OVERWEIGHT

A horse carrying more weight than the conditions of the race require, usually because the jockey exceeds the stated limit.

PADDOCK

Structure or area where horses are saddled and kept before going to the track.

PARI-MUTUEL

System of wagering where all the money is returned to the wagerers after deduction of taxes, track and state percentages.

PAST PERFORMANCES

A horse's racing record, earnings, bloodlines and other data, presented in composite form.

PATROL JUDGE

An official who observe the progress of a race from various vantage points around the track.

PHENYLBUTAZOLIDAN

See "Bute"

PHENYLBUTAZONE

See "Bute"

PHOTO FINISH

A result so close that it is necessary to use the finish-line camera to determine the order of finish.

PILL

Small numbered ball used in a blind draw to decide post positions.

POLES

Markers at measured distances around the track designating the distance from the finish. The quarter pole, for instance, is a quarter of a mile from the finish, not from the start.

POLL

The top of the horse's head, between the ears.

POST PARADE

Horses going from paddock to starting gate past the stands.

POST POSITION

Position of stall in starting gate from which a horse starts.

POST TIME

Designated time for a race to start.

PROP

When a horse suddenly stops moving by digging its front feet into the ground.

PURSE

The total monetary amount distributed after a race to the owners of the entrants who have finished in the top five positions.

QUARTER CRACK

A crack between the toe and heel which can be rectified quite easily by a knowledgeable blacksmith through the use of fiberglass.

RIDGLING ("RIG")

A horse with one or both undescended testes.

RIDDEN OUT

A horse that finishes a race under mild urging, not as severe as driving.

ROAN

Horse with white and red hairs mingled throughout its coat.

ROUTE

A race distance of longer than 1 1/4 miles.

RUN DOWN

Abrasions of the heel that can be easily rectified through the use of "run down wraps".

SADDLE

A Thoroughbred racing saddle is the lightest saddle used, weighing less than two pounds.

SCALE OF WEIGHTS

Fixed weights to be carried by horses according to their age, sex, race distance and time of year.

SCRATCH

To be taken out of a race before it starts. Trainers usually scratch horses due to adverse track conditions or a horse's adverse health. A veterinarian can scratch a horse at any time.

SESAMOID BONES

Two small bones (medial and lateral sesamoids) located above and at the back of the fetlock joint. Four common fractures of the sesamoids are apical (along the top of the bone), abaxial (the side of the sesamoid away from the ankle joint), mid-body (sesamoid broken in half) and basilar (through the bottom) fractures.

SHADOW ROLL

A roll (usually sheepskin) that is secured over the bridge of a horse's nose to keep it from seeing shadows on the track and shying away from or jumping them.

SHEDROW

Stable area. A row of barns.
SILKS

Jacket and cap worn by jockeys.
SIRE

Father of a foal.
SLOPPY TRACK

A racing strip that is saturated with water; with standing water visible.
SLOW TRACK

A racing strip that is wet on both the surface and base.
SOFT TRACK

Condition of a turf course with a large amount of moisture. Horses sink very deeply into it.
SOPHOMORES

Three-year-old horses. Called sophomores because age three is the second year of racing eligibility.
SPIT THE BIT

A term referring to a tired horse that begins to run less aggressively, backing off on the "pull" a rider normally feels on the reins from an eager horse. Also used as a generic term for an exhausted horse.
SPLINT

1: Either of the two small bones that lie along the sides of the cannon bone. 2: The condition where calcification occurs on the splint bone causing a bump. This can result from response to a fracture or other irritation to the splint bone.

SPRINT (race)

Short race, less than one mile, typically referred to when dealing with distances of 6 or 7 furlongs. Although, a race contested around one turn, at a mile, is also considered a sprint.

STAKES

A race for which the owner usually must pay a fee to run a horse. The fees, to which the track adds more money to make up the total purse, can be for nominating, maintaining eligibility, entering and starting. Stakes races by invitation require no fees.

STALLION

Retired male horse that now spends his days breeding to mares.

STEADIED

A horse being taken in hand by its rider, usually because of being in close quarters.

STEWARDS

Officials of the race meeting responsible for enforcing the rules of racing.

STIRRUPS

Metal "D"-shaped rings into which a jockey places his/her feet. They can be raised or lowered depending on the jockey's preference. Also known as "irons."

STRETCH TURN

Bend of track into the final straightaway.

STUD

Stallion.

TAKEN UP

A horse pulled up sharply by its rider because of being in close quarters.

TATTOO

A permanent, indelible mark on the inside of the upper lip used to identify the horse.

THOROUGHBRED

A Thoroughbred is a horse whose parentage traces back to any of the three "founding sires": the Darley Arabian, Byerly Turk and Godolphin Barb, and who has satisfied the rules and requirements of The Jockey Club and is registered in The American Stud Book or in a foreign stud book recognized by The Jockey Club and the International Stud Book Committee.

TONGUE TIE or STRAP

Strip of cloth-type material used to stabilize a horse's tongue to prevent the horse from "choking down" in a race or workout or to keep the tongue from sliding up over the bit, rendering the horse uncontrollable.

TURN DOWN (otherwise known as "quarter-inch bends")

Rear shoe that is turned down 1/4-inch to one inch at the ends to provide better traction on an off-track. Illegal in many jurisdictions.

TURF COURSE

Grass covered race course.

UNDERLAY

Horse whose odds are more promising than his potential to win.

VALET

A person who helps jockeys keep their wardrobe and equipment in order.

WALKOVER

A race in which only one horse competes.

WASHED OUT

A horse that becomes so nervous that it sweats profusely. Also known as "washy" or "lathered (up)."

WEANLING

A foal that is less than one-year-old that has been separated (weaned) from its dam.

WEIGHT

The assigned weight for a horse, including the jockey, equipment and lead weights if needed.

WHITE

An extremely rare horse color in which all the hairs are white. The horse's eyes are brown, not pink, as would be the case for an albino.

WITHERS

Area above the shoulder, where the neck meets the back.

WORKOUT

Exercise session at a predetermined distance.

YEARLING

A horse that is one year old. The universal birth date of horses is January 1.

YIELDING

Condition of a turf course with a great deal of moisture. Horses sink into it noticeably.

THE END

Made in the USA